1000
Great Motifs
for Crafters

Alan D. Gear & Barry L. Freestone

COLLINS & BROWN

First published in Great Britain in 2003 by
Collins & Brown
151 Freston Road
London, W10 6TH

Copyright © Collins & Brown Limited 2003
Text copyright © Alan D. Gear and
Barry L. Freestone 2001
Illustrations copyright © Collins & Brown Limited
2003

Distributed in the United States and Canada by
Sterling Publishing Co. 387 Park Avenue South,
New York, NY 10016, USA

10 9 8 7 6 5 4

A CIP catalogue record for this book is available
from the British Library.

ISBN 10: 1-843403-95-1
ISBN 13: 978-1-843403-95-1

Conceived, edited and designed by
Collins & Brown Limited

Editor and designer: Kate Haxell
Illustrations: Kuo Kang Chen, Dominic Harris
and Kate Simunek

Reproduction by Classicscan Pte Ltd
Printed and bound by CT Printing, China

This book can be ordered direct from the publisher.
Contact the marketing department, but try your
bookshop first.

www.anovabooks.com

ABOUT THIS BOOK

Through our television shows, our teaching workshops and our stands at international craft fairs, we come into contact with experts in every field of crafts. Embroiderers, stampers, potters, stencillers, beaders, painters, stitchers, glass painters, knitters… the list goes on and on, and proves that the interest in both traditional and new crafts has never been greater than it is now.

One thing that all of these crafters have in common is that they need designs to work with. For many crafters this can be a constant source of frustration: finding the right motif to suit your vision for a particular project can be time-consuming and, all too often, can end in an unsatisfactory compromise.

Two years ago, in response to this need for interesting and stylish motifs, we published our first motif library. Although we knew that such a book was needed, we were still amazed by the positive response from the many crafters who contacted us.

So, to satisfy all of those who asked for yet more motifs, here is another motif library packed with 1000 new motifs. The book is organized into easy-to-use categories and within these are sub-categories. Every motif in every category has an individual reference number, so once you have found the perfect motif, it is easy to find it again and again.

Whether you are a cross-stitcher looking for a design to celebrate Christmas, a painter searching for the perfect motif for a children's nursery or a stamper needing a floral pattern for a greetings card, you will find something to suit you. In fact, no matter what your favourite craft is, we hope that you will find what you need within the pages of this book

All the motifs are black-line artworks, ready for you to use. Some motifs may be more suitable for some crafts than others, so in every section there is a selection to choose from. In addition, at the front of the book there is a techniques section, including advice on how to enlarge and reduce motifs to fit your projects and how to transfer the motifs onto soft and hard materials.

You will also find illustrations and tips on using motifs for different crafts. There just isn't the space to illustrate using motifs for every craft that exists, but you will find a representative selection here.

We hope you enjoy using this book and that the motifs within it will inspire you for years to come.

Alan D. Gear and Barry L. Freestone

CONTENTS

ENLARGING A MOTIF

The simplest way of enlarging or reducing a motif in size is on a photocopier. Decide on the size you want the finished design to be and then measure the motif in the book. Divide the desired size by the actual size and multiply this number by 100 to get the percentage you need to enlarge the motif by. If you don't have access to a photocopier, then you can use the grid technique shown here.

 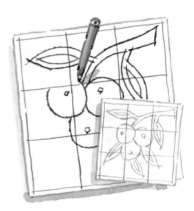

Step 1

On a piece of tracing paper the size of the original motif, draw a grid of 1cm (½in) squares. Lay the tracing paper over the motif and use small pieces of masking tape along the edges to hold it in place. If the motif is very detailed, you may need to make the squares smaller.

Step 2

On a plain piece of paper the size you want the motif to be, draw another grid. This grid should have the same number of squares, but they should be proportionately larger. Copy the lines from the tracing-paper grid onto the larger grid, square by square. You can also reduce a motif this way by making the squares of the plain paper grid smaller than those of the original grid.

TRANSFERRING A MOTIF

To transfer a motif onto a variety of materials, first trace it off accurately onto a piece of plain paper, or photocopy it. If necessary, enlarge or reduce the motif to the desired size (see page 8) before transferring it onto your chosen material. If you are working on a material that is not washable or is expensive, practice the appropriate transferring technique on a scrap piece before embarking on the project.

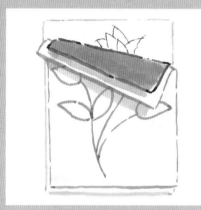

Transferring a motif onto hard materials

Use carbon paper to transfer a motif onto a variety of materials including glass, mirror glass, wood, pottery, plaster and patterned or textured paper and cardboard. Place the carbon paper face down on the surface you want the motif to appear on, lay the motif over the top and then draw over the lines with a ballpoint pen.

Transferring a motif onto fabric or canvas

Special dressmaker's carbon paper is available in haberdashery and sewing shops and can be used in the same way as ordinary carbon paper to transfer a motif onto fabric.

To transfer a motif onto canvas for needlepoint, draw a central cross across the motif and the canvas. Lay the canvas over the motif, aligning the two crosses, then draw over the lines with a waterproof pen.

If you are working cross stitch, it's better to transfer the motif onto chart paper rather than directly onto the canvas. Chart paper is available in haberdashery and sewing shops. Lay the chart paper over the motif on a lightbox, or tape them to a window, so that you can see the lines clearly. Lightly draw over the motif lines in pencil. To produce a chart carefully remove the motif and colour in the appropriate squares in the colours you want to stitch in.

NEEDLEPOINT

Tent stitch is the most commonly used needlepoint stitch and will reproduce quite fine detail. If you are working on a large design, use a frame to prevent the fabric distorting while you stitch.

CROSS STITCH

This is worked over a counted number of threads, usually two threads though the number can vary depending on how detailed the design is. Use a hoop to hold the fabric taut while you work.

To work tent stitch, take the needle diagonally under two intersections of the canvas, keeping the tops of the stitches in line. Work from right to left across the canvas, turning it around at the start of every new row. This stitch allows you to cover all of the canvas, though if you are worried about some canvas showing, you can paint the design onto the canvas with appropriately coloured acrylic paints before you start stitching.

The diagonal stitches should always slant the same way, though it doesn't matter which one (upper or lower) slants which way. The stitches can be worked in two ways: either the whole stitch can be worked before moving on to the next one (see top diagram), or all the diagonals slanting one way can be worked along a row, then all the diagonals slanting the other way (see centre and bottom diagrams).

FREEHAND EMBROIDERY

This type of embroidery does not require a chart, just transfer the motif straight onto the fabric. Use a hoop to hold the fabric taut while you stitch.

MACHINE EMBROIDERY

Back the fabric with interfacing or tear-away stabilizer to help stop it puckering. When working on a small, detailed area, use a hoop to keep the fabric taut.

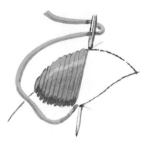

As there is such a wide range of embroidery stitches to choose from, any motif, no matter how detailed, can be reproduced in embroidery. An outline can be rendered in a stitch such as split, running, feather or chain stitch. Areas of the motif can be filled in with satin stitch (see above), or long-and-short stitch. Additional detail can be added with knots and decorative stitches such as sheaf or lazy daisy stitch.

Simple machine embroidery (see above) uses an ordinary presser foot and a variety of different stitches, depending on what the sewing machine can do. Quite detailed designs can be worked this way, though negotiating tight curves smoothly can be tricky. Alternatively you can drop the feeder teeth and remove the presser foot and use the machine like a drawing tool. This is a versatile technique, but it needs practice.

APPLIQUÉ

Motifs with straight lines or gentle curves are best suited to this technique, unless you are using a non-fraying fabric, or one backed with interfacing, and therefore do not have to roll the edges under.

BEADING

This couched beading technique offers a quick way to bead an outline. You can also use it to fill in a shape, but you need to plan the design carefully first. Use a hoop to keep the fabric taut.

Cut out a motif and draw around it on the wrong side of the fabric. Cut out the fabric shape leaving a 5mm (¼in) hem allowance all round. Tack the shape to the background fabric, keeping the stitches 1.5cm (¾in) in from the edges. Cut off any outward corners and snip into any inward ones. Stitch the shapes in place using an outlining embroidery stitch. As you work, use the point of the needle to roll under the hem allowance.

Thread a beading needle with beading thread and knot the end. Bring the needle up at one corner of the motif. Thread on more beads than you need and lay them along the outline of the motif. Thread a sewing needle and knot the end. Bring it up between the first two beads and make a tiny stitch over the beading thread. Repeat this after every bead to hold them all in place. Slide any excess beads off the thread and secure it on the back.

PAINTING

Using a motif from this book means that you do not have to be artistic to paint a design. Fabric, wood, pottery, glass, papier mâché – almost any material can be painted with the right paints.

DÉCOUPAGE

Photocopy appropriate motifs onto coloured or patterned paper. The paper should not be too thick or the paper shapes will be proud of the surface. Choose a clear, satin-finish varnish to seal the work.

Before you start a project, experiment on a scrap piece of the material you are going to paint. Try using different paintbrushes to produce different weights and styles of line. Fine brushes with long bristles are best for painting lines, while thicker, soft brushes are suitable for filling in areas. Square-ended brushes are useful for painting borders or simple geometric shapes and stencilling brushes produce neat dots.

You can also photocopy motifs onto white paper and then decorate them with smudge-proof media, such as pencils or paint. Seal them with PVA glue. Cut out the motifs and arrange them on the background. Make tiny pencil marks at the corners of the shapes so that you can re-position them accurately. Brush PVA over the surface and stick the shapes in place. When the glue is completely dry, brush at least three coats of varnish over the surface.

STENCILLING

Not all motifs are appropriate for stencilling, though many can be adapted for this technique. To work as a stencil a motif has to be broken down into separate shapes that are held together with tiny 'bridges'. These 'bridges' can vary in size and shape and the more sensitively positioned within the design they are, the better the stencil will look. Plan the stencil on plain paper first before transferring it onto stencil card.

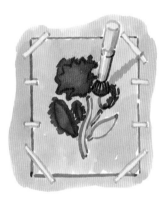

Step 1

Working on a cutting mat, use a sharp craft knife to carefully cut out the separate sections of the motif. Hold the knife nearly upright and slowly cut towards yourself, working from the centre of the design out towards the edges. Use your other hand to hold the stencil card still on the mat, but make sure you keep your fingers out of the way of the knife.

Step 2

Using low-tack masking tape or spray glue, stick the stencil to the surface you want to decorate. Spread some paint out on a palette and dab just the very tips of the bristles of a stencilling brush into it. Dab off excess paint on the side of the palette. Holding the brush upright, dab the bristles down onto the stencil, covering all of the cut-out areas. Carefully lift the stencil off the surface.

STAMPING

Stamps can be cut from many different materials, including potatoes, thick cardboard and lino tiles. Sponge, however, is one of the most commonly used materials as it is readily available, comes in different densities and finishes and can be used to make quite detailed stamps. A bath sponge will add texture to a stamped design, while high-density foam works well with detailed motifs.

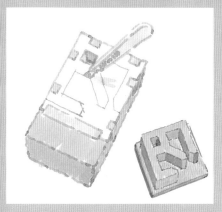

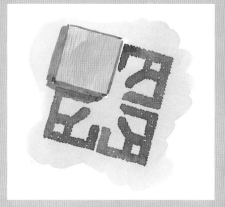

Step 1

Trace or photocopy a motif and stick it to the top of a sponge with masking tape. Using a sharp craft knife, carefully cut along the outlines, cutting through the paper and sponge at the same time. To make the stamp easier to use, cut a small piece of wood, MDF or thick cardboard to mount it on. Stick the cut-out sponge shape to this backing with contact adhesive (see small picture).

Step 2

A simple stamp can be used to make more complicated patterns and borders by rotating and repeating the image. Choose a paint that is appropriate for the material you want to stamp and practice first on a scrap piece. Spread paint out on a palette and press the stamp evenly onto it. Press it evenly onto the material and lift the stamp straight up off the surface to avoid smudging the design.

1a.1

1a.2

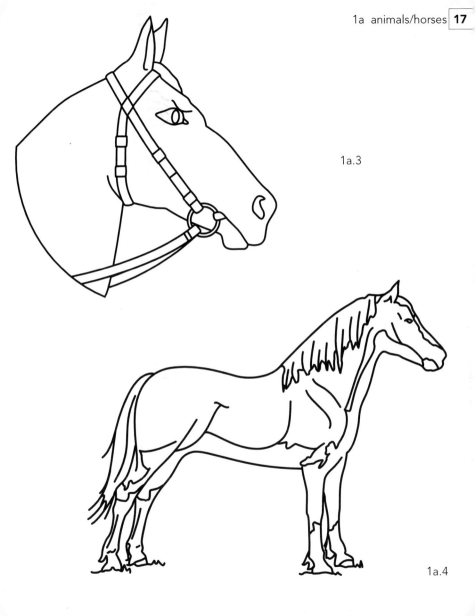

1a.3

1a.4

1b.1

1b.2

1b.3

1b.4

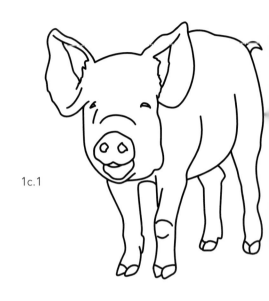

1c.1

1c.2

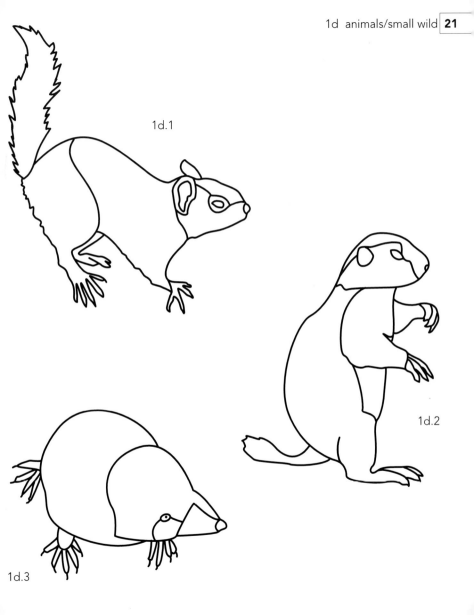

1d.1

1d.2

1d.3

1e.1

1e.2

1f.1

1f.2

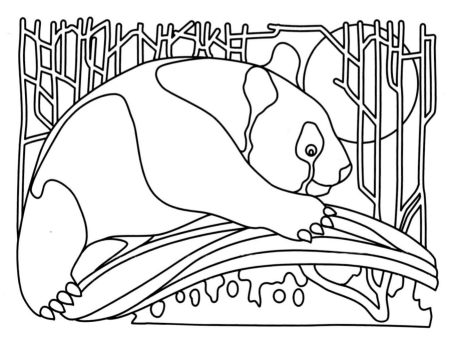

1g.1

1g.2

1g.3

1g.4

1h.1

1h.2

1i.1

1i.2

1i.3

1i.4

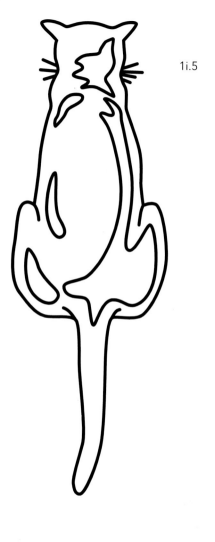

1i.5

1i.6

1j.1

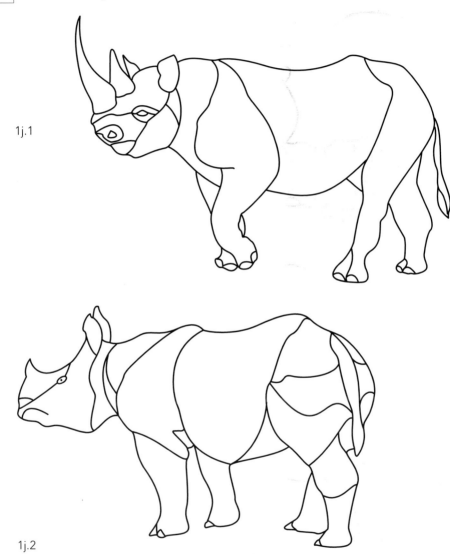

1j.2

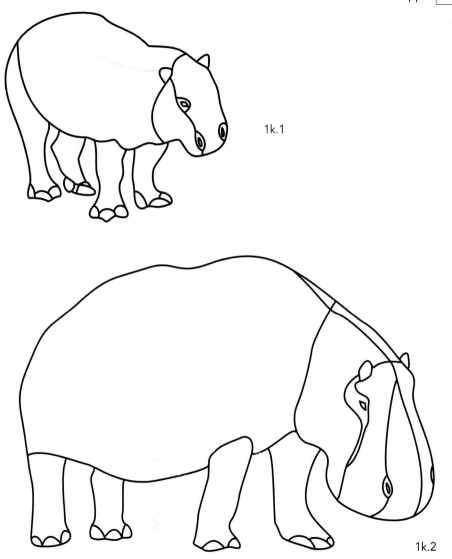

1k.1

1k.2

1l.1

1l.2

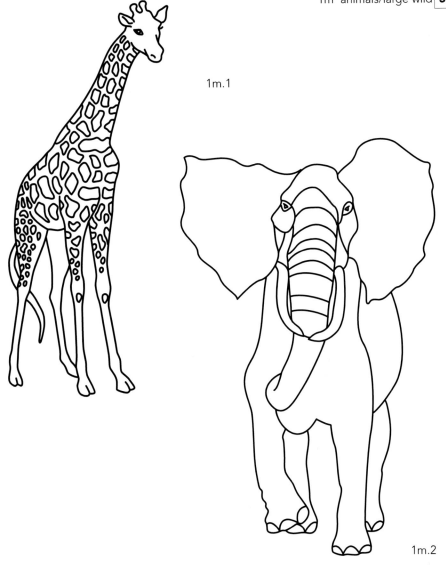

1m.1

1m.2

1m.3

1m.4

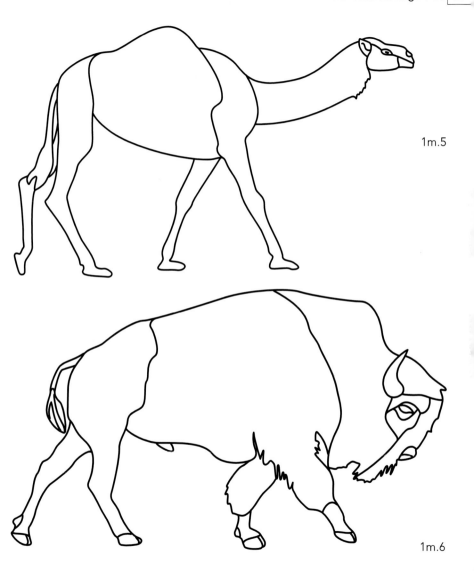

1m.5

1m.6

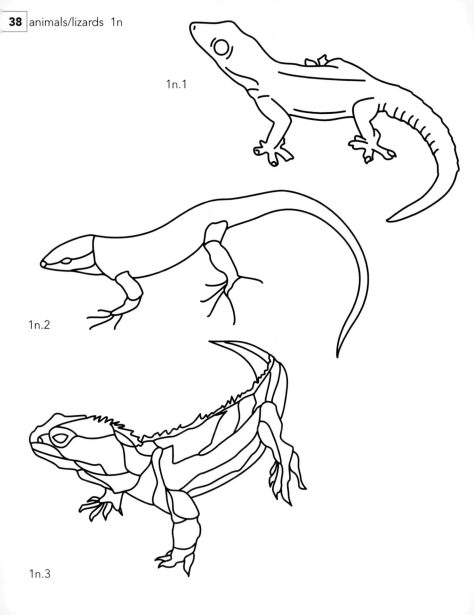

1n.1

1n.2

1n.3

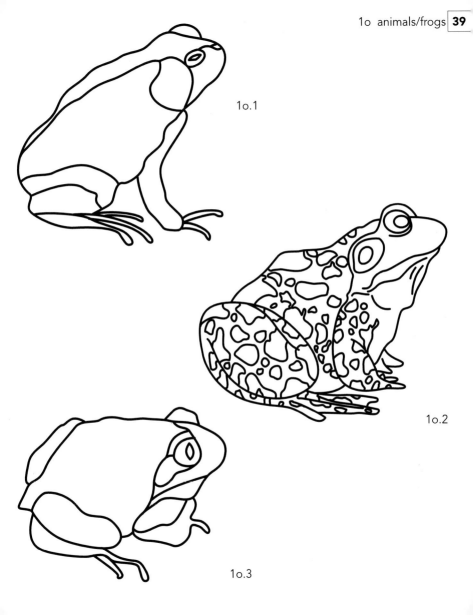

1o.1

1o.2

1o.3

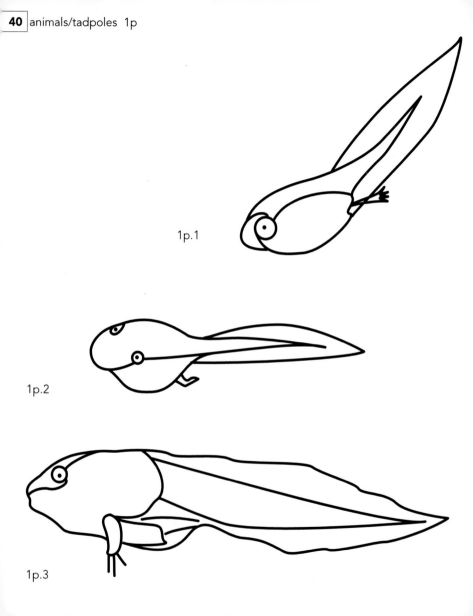

1p.1

1p.2

1p.3

1q.1

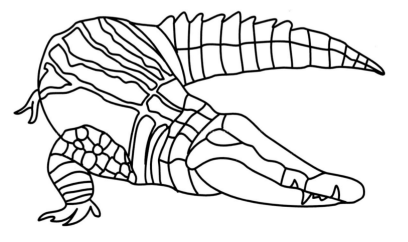

1q.2

1r.1

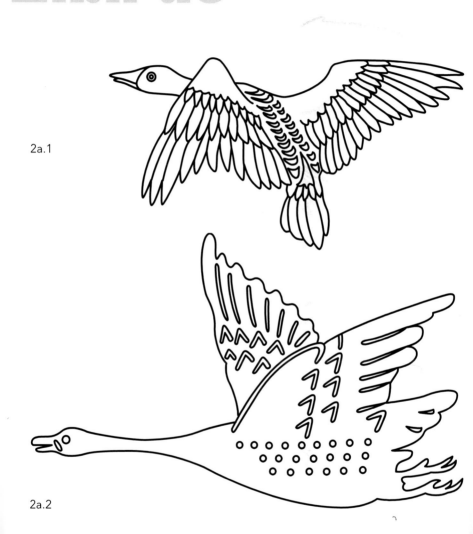

2a.1

2a.2

2a.3

2a.4

2a.5

2a.6

2a.7

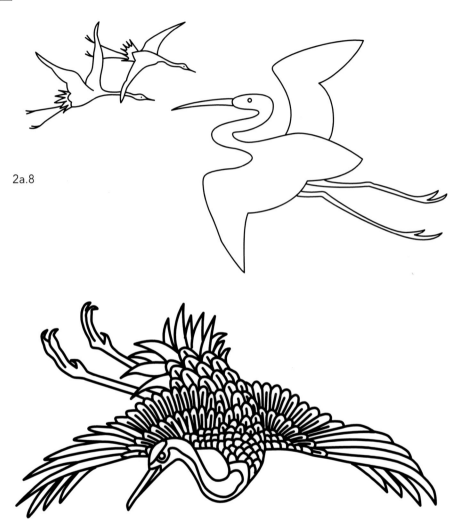

2a.8

2a.9

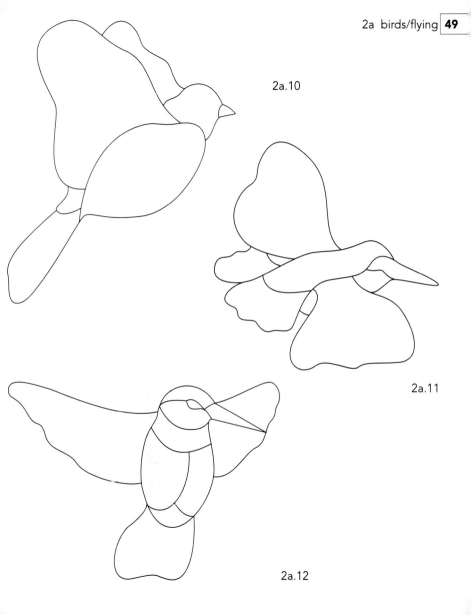

2a.10

2a.11

2a.12

2a.13

2a.14

2a.15

2a.16

2b.1

2b.2

2b.3

2b.4

2c.1

2c.2

2c.3

2c.4

2c.5

2c.6

2c.7

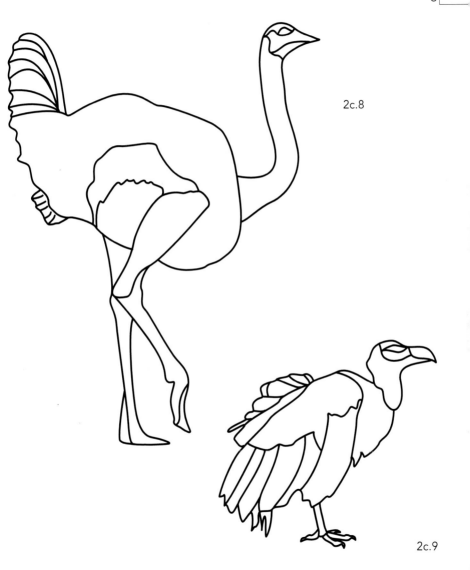

2c.8

2c.9

2c.10

2c.11

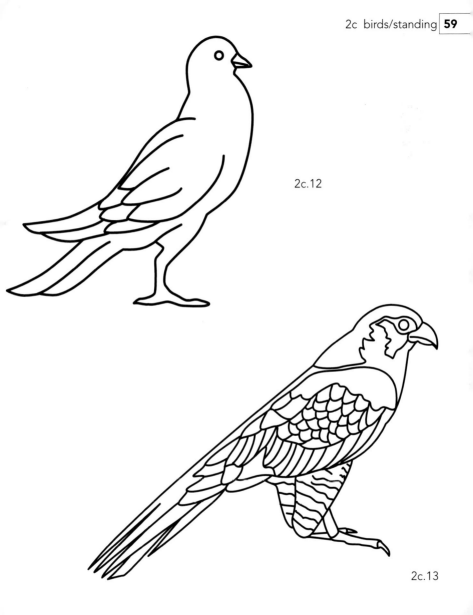

2c.12

2c.13

2c.14

2c.15

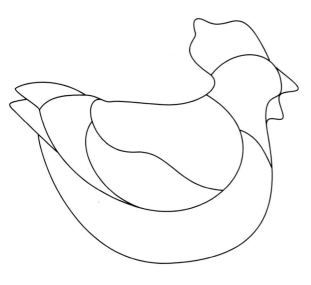

2d.1

2d.2

2d.3

2d.4

2d.5

2e.1

2e.2

2e.3

2e.4

2f.1

2f.2

2g.1

2g.2

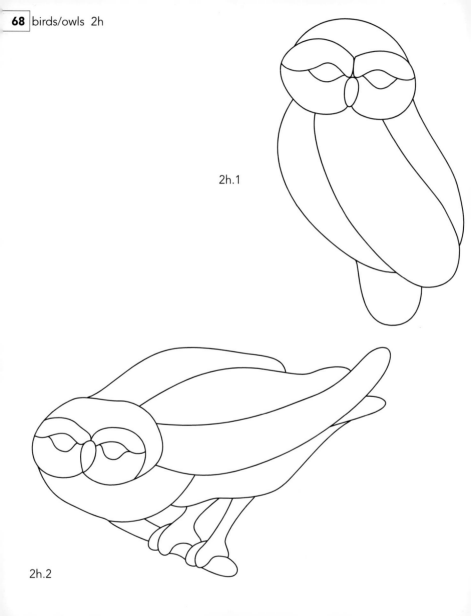

2h.1

2h.2

2h.3

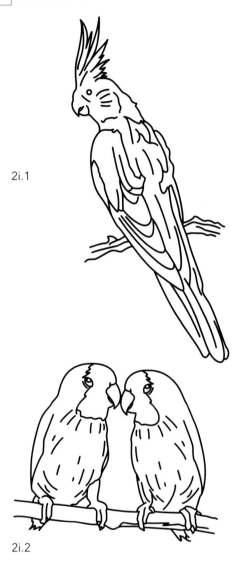

2i.1

2i.2

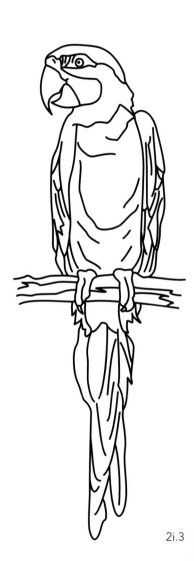

2i.3

2j.1

2j.3

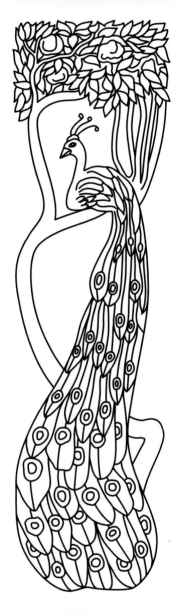

2j.4

2k.1

2k.2

2k.3

2l.1

2l.2

21.3

21.4

21.5

21.6

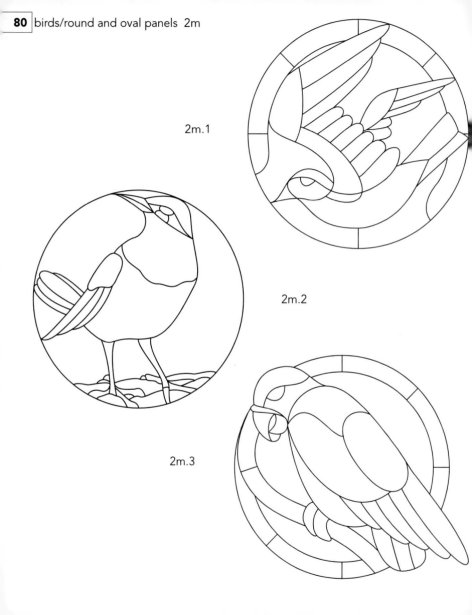

2m.1

2m.2

2m.3

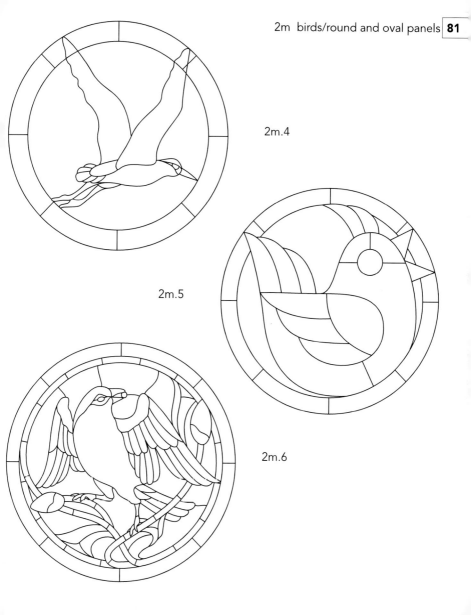

2m.4

2m.5

2m.6

82 birds/round and oval panels 2m

2m.7

2m.8

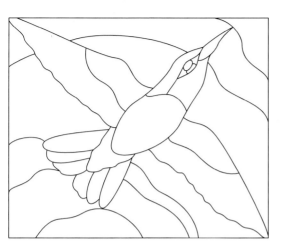

2n.1

2n.2

2n.3

2n.4

2n.5

2o.1

2o.2

2o.3

2o.4

2p.1

2p.2

2p.3

2p.4

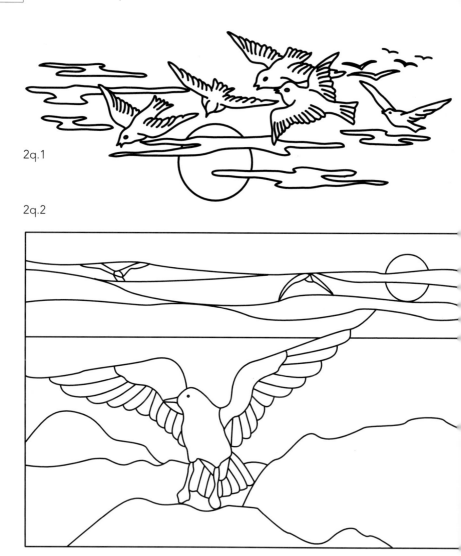

2q.1

2q.2

2q.3

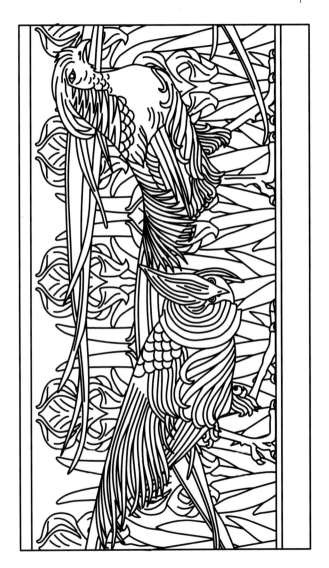

2q.5

3.insects

3a.1

3a.2

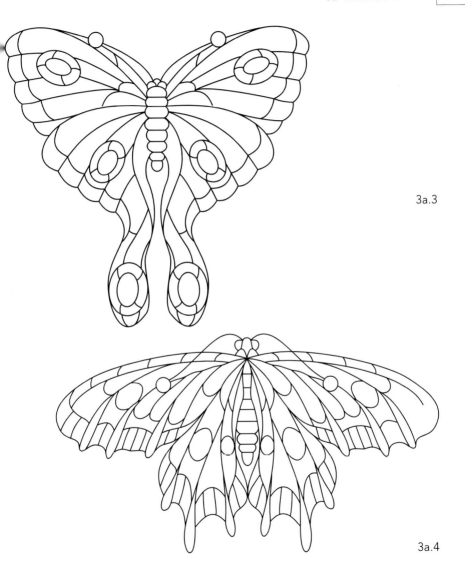

3a.3

3a.4

3a.5

3a.6

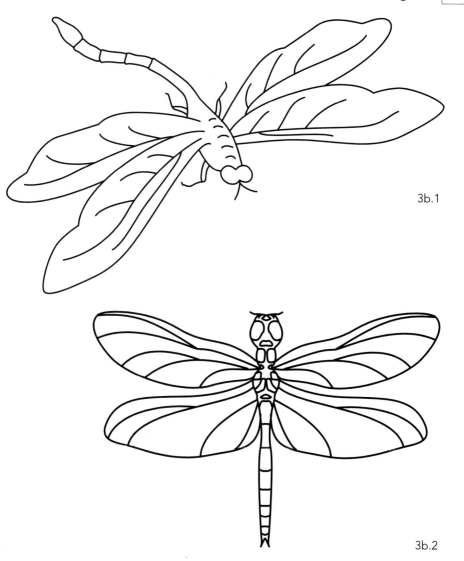

3b.1

3b.2

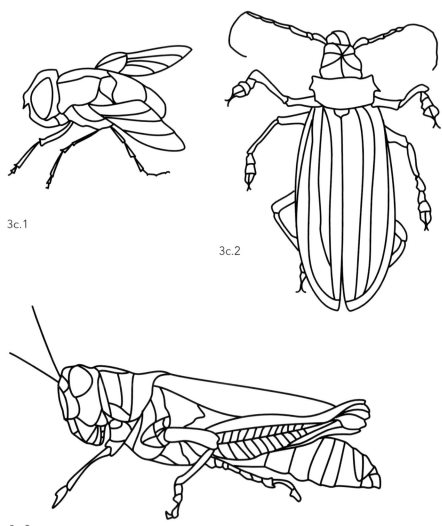

3c.1

3c.2

3c.3

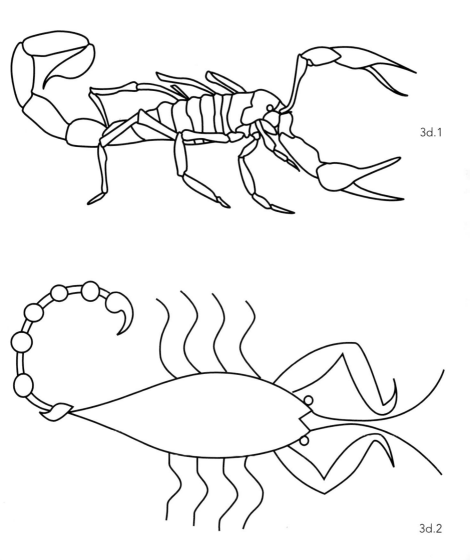

3d.1

3d.2

3e.1

3e.2

3e.3

3e.4

3e.5

3e.6

3e.7

4.seashore

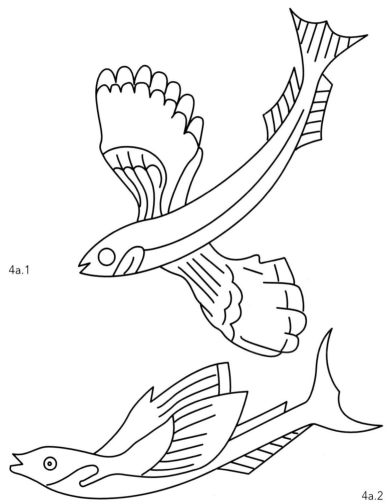

4a.1

4a.2

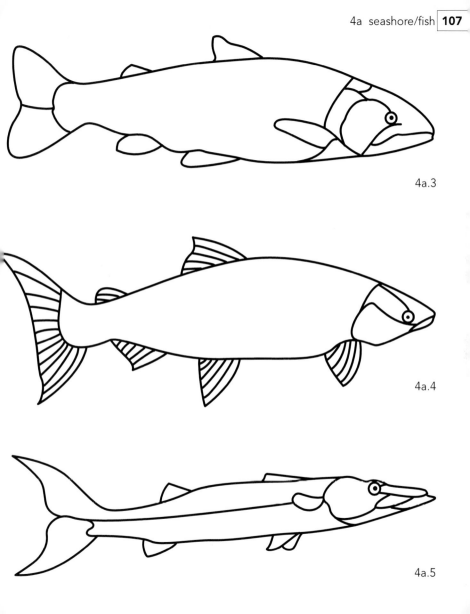

4a.3

4a.4

4a.5

4a.6

4a.7

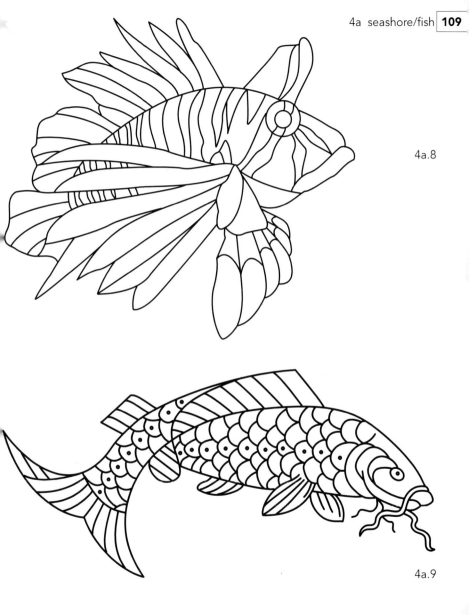

4a.8

4a.9

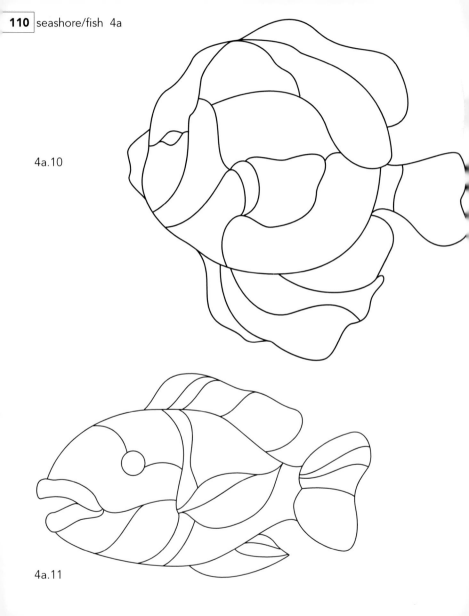

4a.10

4a.11

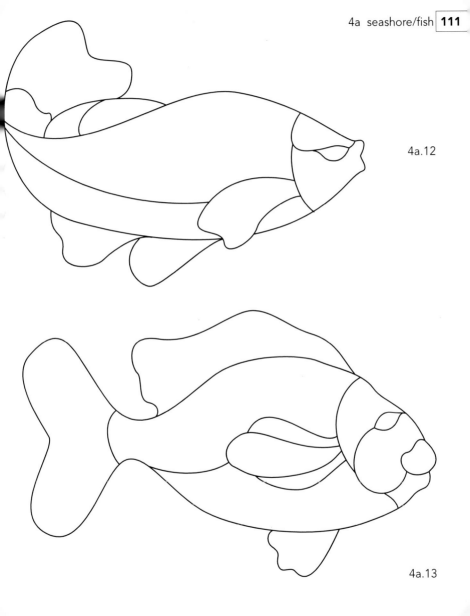

4a.12

4a.13

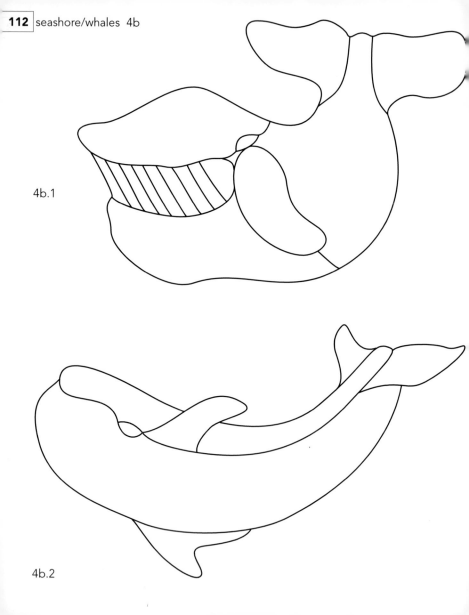

4b.1

4b.2

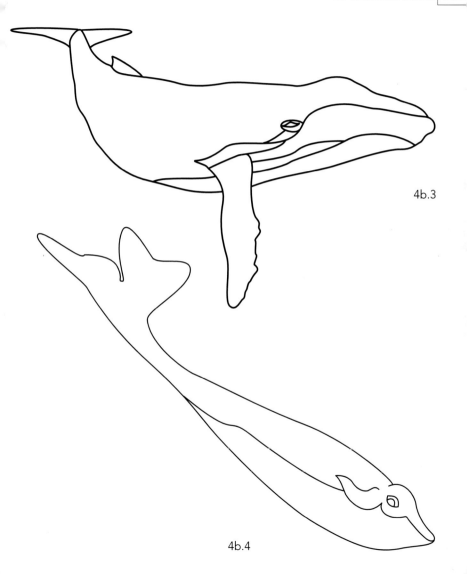

4b.3

4b.4

4c.1

4c.2

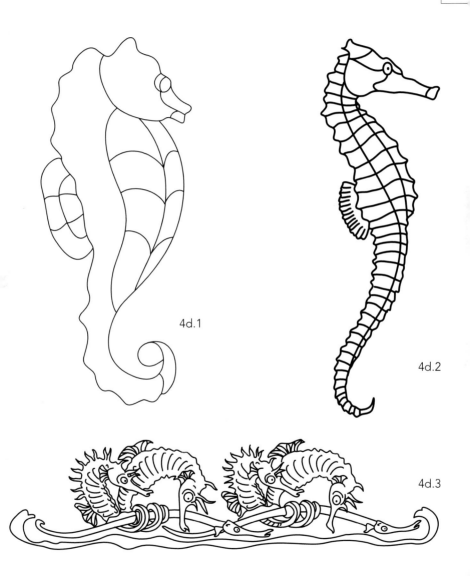

4d.1

4d.2

4d.3

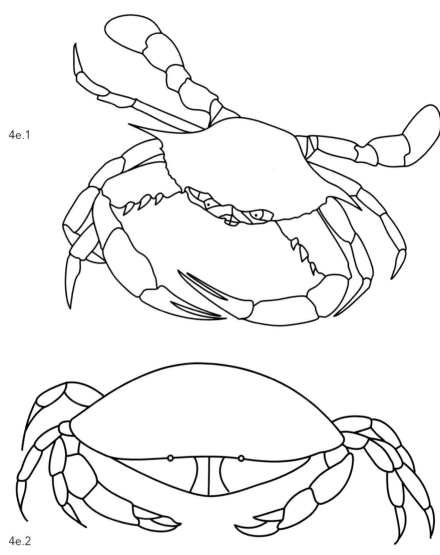

4e.1

4e.2

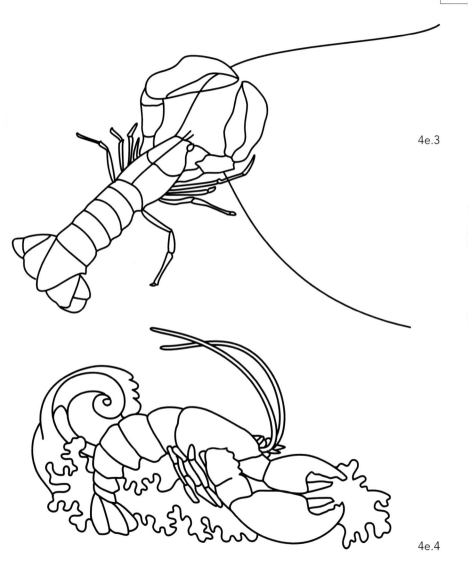

4e.3

4e.4

4f.1

4f.2

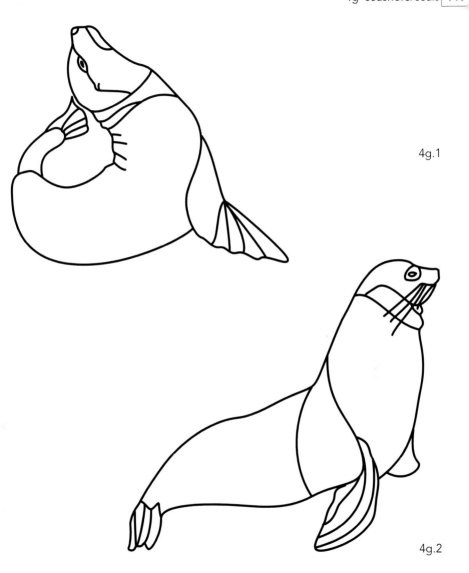

4g.1

4g.2

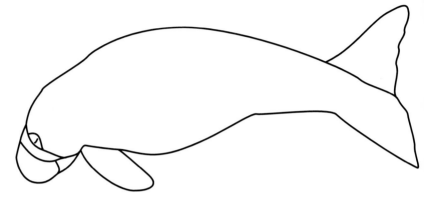

4h.1

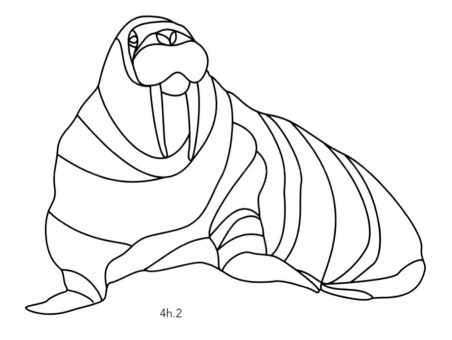

4h.2

4i.1

4i.2

4i.3

4i.4

4i.5

4i.6

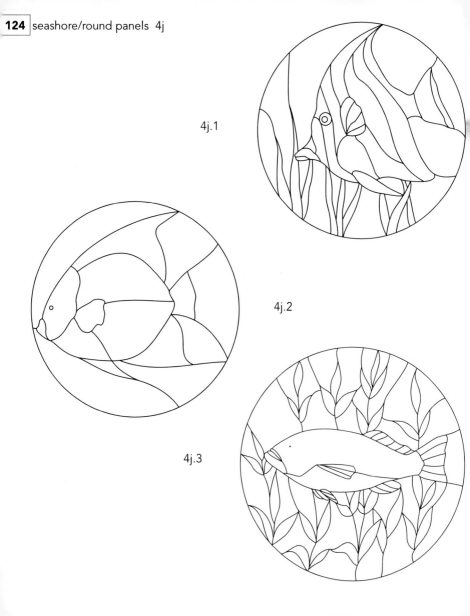

4j.1

4j.2

4j.3

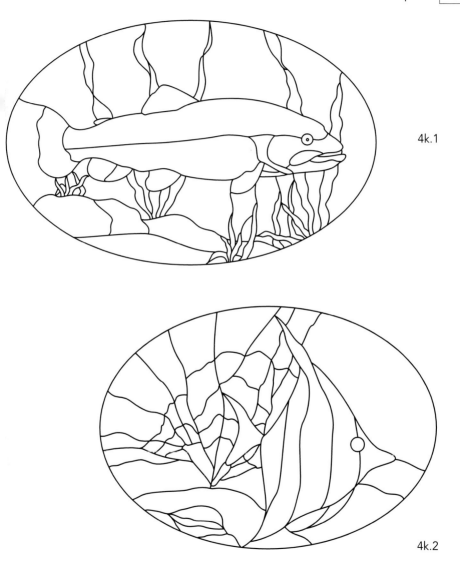

4k.1

4k.2

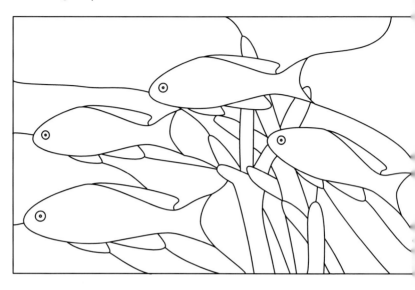

4l.1

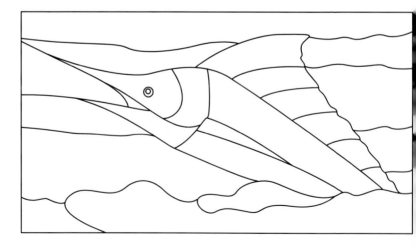

4l.2

4m.1

4m.2

5.people

5a.1

5a.2

5a.3

5a.4

5a.5

5a.6

5a.7

5a.8

5a.9

5a.10

5a.11

5a.12

5a.13

5a.14

5a.15

5b.1

5b.2

5b.3

5b.5

5b.4

5b.6

5c.1

5c.2

5d.1

5d.2

5d.3

5d.4

5e.1

5e.2

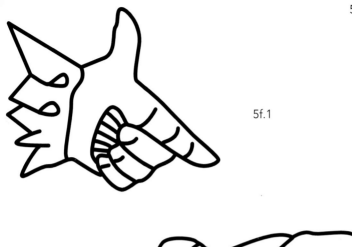

5f.1

5f.2

5f.3

5g.1

5g.2

5h.1

5h.2

5h.3

5h.4

5h.5

5h.6

5i.1

5i.2

5i.3

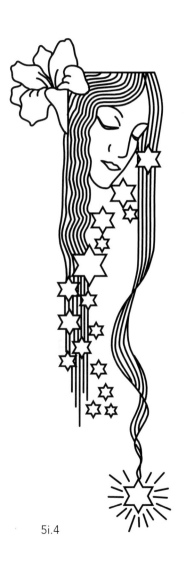

5i.4

5j.1

5j.2

5j.3

5j.4

6a.1

6a.2

6a.3

6a.4

6a.5

6a.6

6a.7

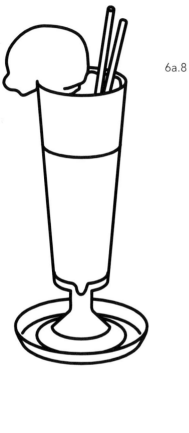

6a.8

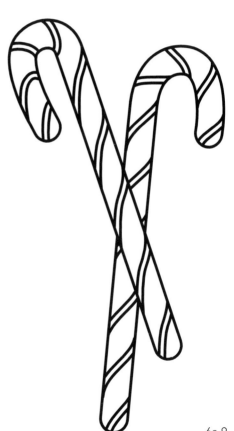

6a.9

6a.10

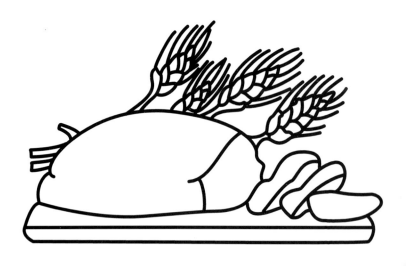

6a.11

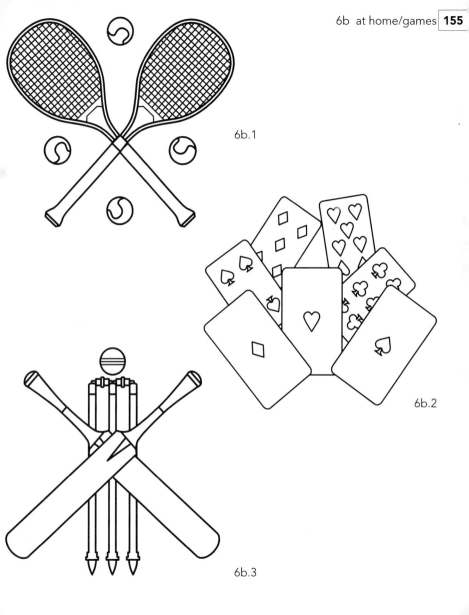

6b.1

6b.2

6b.3

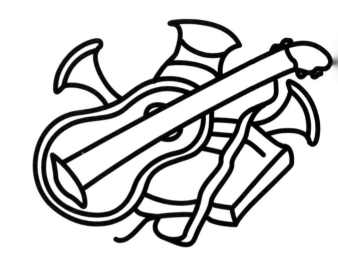

6c.1

6c.2

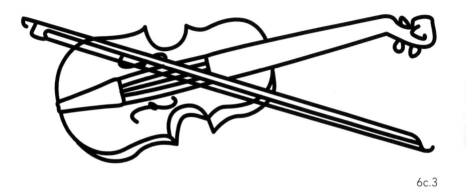

6c.3

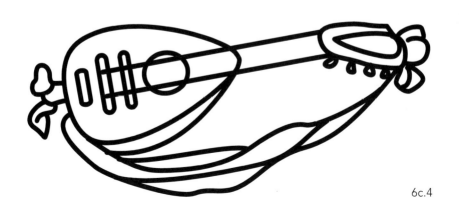

6c.4

6c.5

6c.6

6c.7

6c.8

6c.9

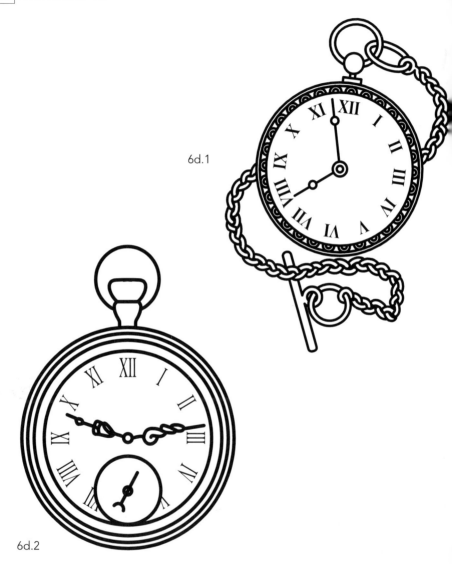

6d.1

6d.2

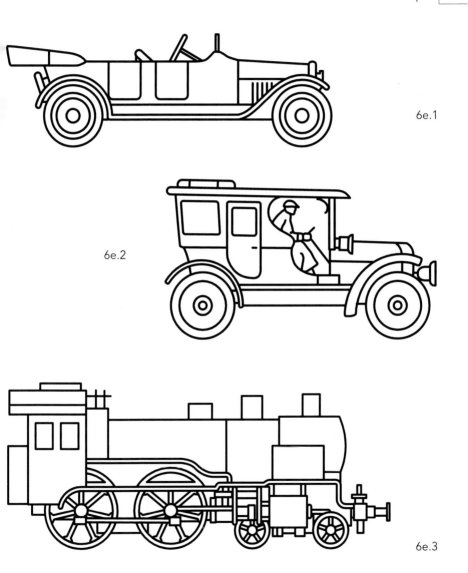

6e.1

6e.2

6e.3

7.celebrations

7a.1

7a.2

7a.3

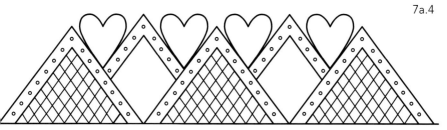

7a.4

7a.5

7b.1

7b.2

7b.3

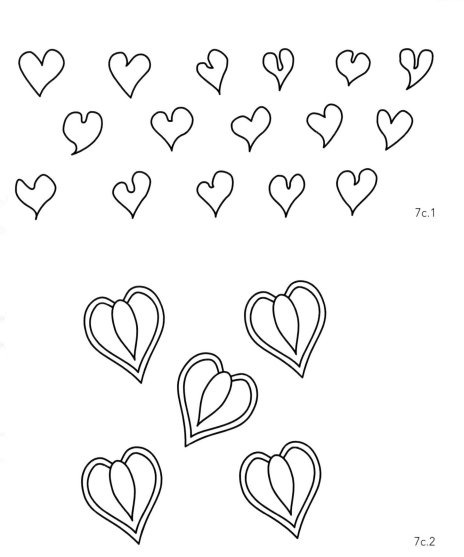

7c.1

7c.2

7d.1

7d.2

7d.3

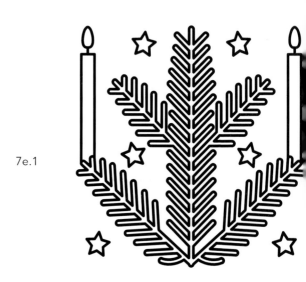

7e.1

7e.2

7e.3

7e.4

7e.5

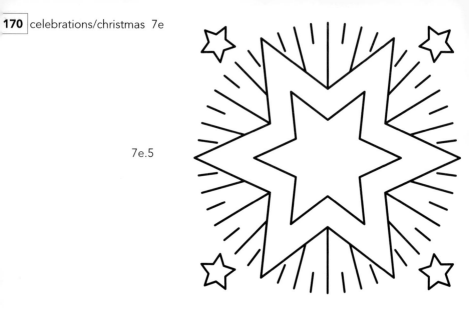

7e.6

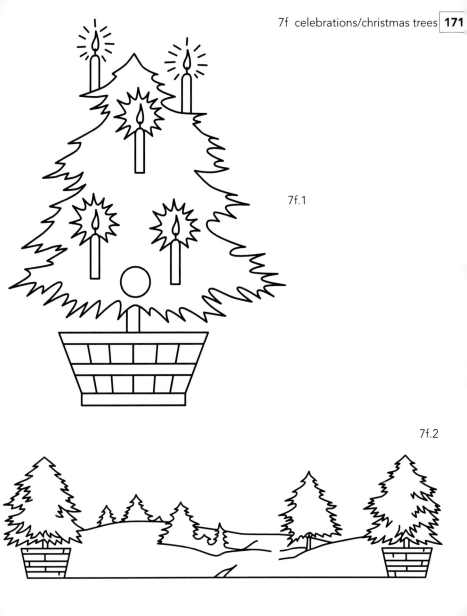

7f.1

7f.2

7g.1

7g.2

7h.1

7h.2

7h.3

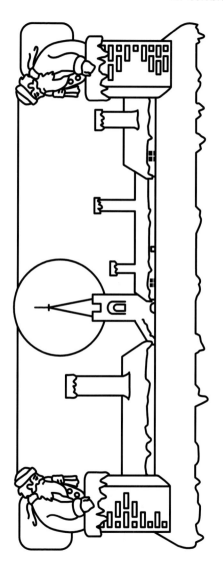

7h.4

7i.1

7i.2

7i.3

8.flowers

8a.1

8a.2

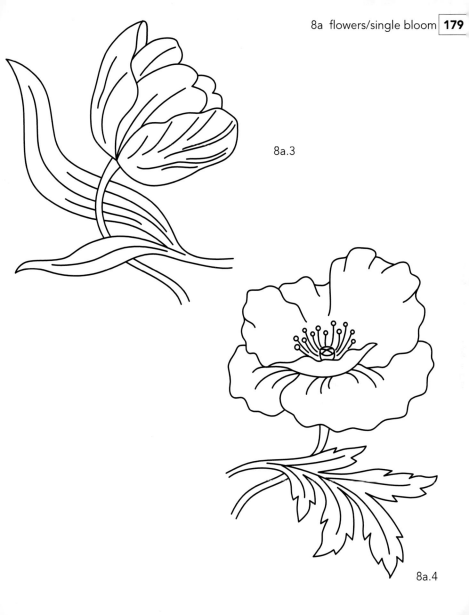

8a.3

8a.4

8a.5

8a.6

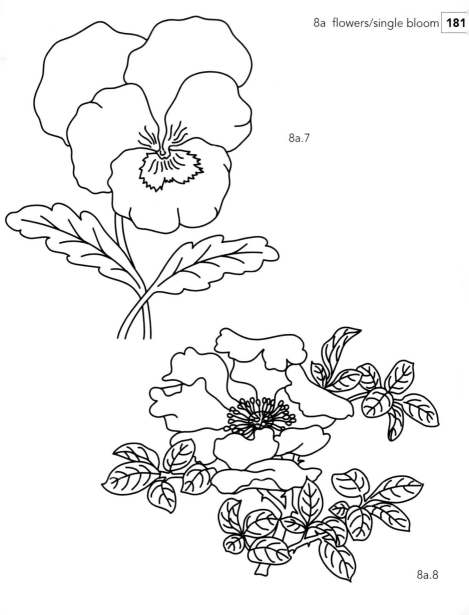

8a.7

8a.8

8b.1

8b.2

8b.3

8b.4

8b.5

8b.6

8b.7

8b.8

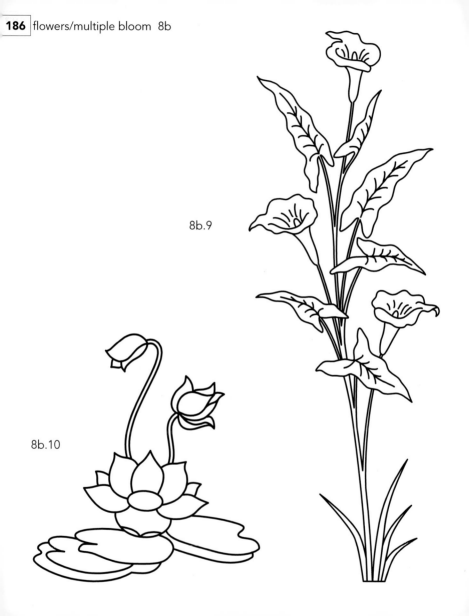

8b.9

8b.10

8b.11

8b.12

8b.13

8b.14

8b.15

8b.16

8b.17

8b.18

8b.19

8b.22

8b.23

8b.24

8b.25

8b.26

8b.27

8c.1

8c.2

8c.3   8c.4   8c.5

8c.7

8c.8

8c.9

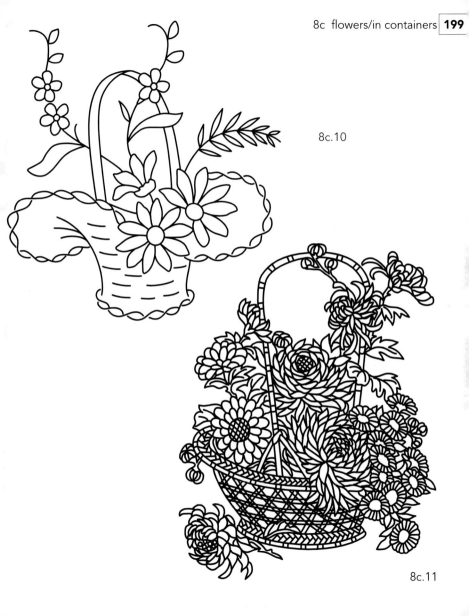

8c.10

8c.11

8c.12

8c.13

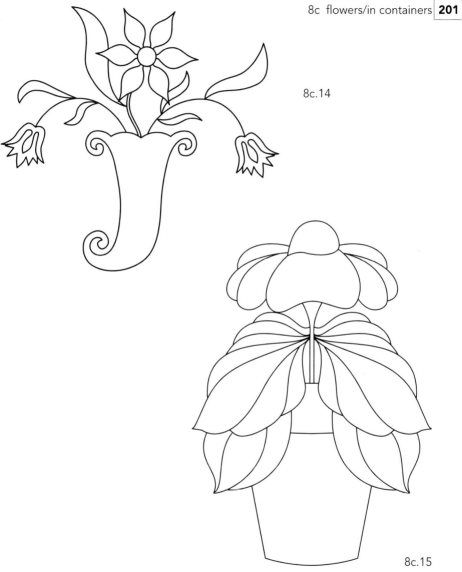

8c.14

8c.15

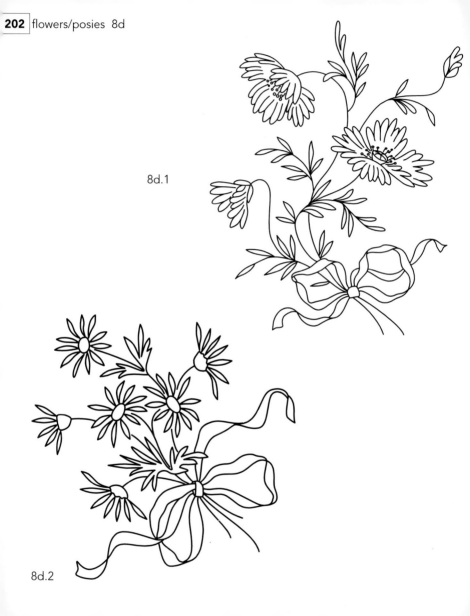

8d.1

8d.2

8d.3

8e.1

8e.2

8e.3

8f.1

8f.2

8f.3

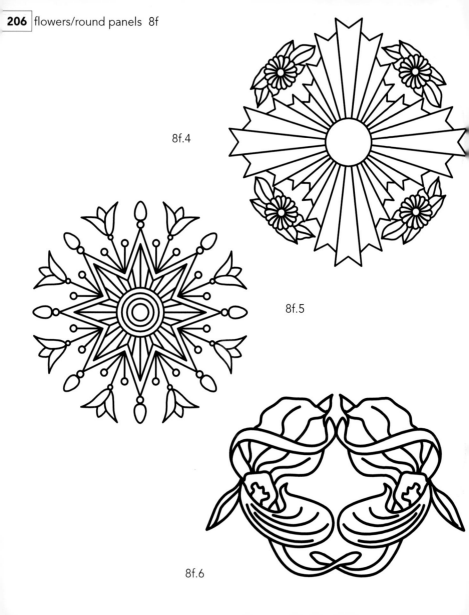

8f.4

8f.5

8f.6

8f.7

8f.8

8f.9

8f.10

8f.11

8f.12

8f.13

8f.14

8f.15

8g.1

8g.2

8g.4

8g.5

8g.6

8g.7

8g.8

8g.9

8g.10

8g.11

8g.12

8g.13

8g.14

8g.15

8g.16

8g.17

8h.1

8h.2

8h.3

8h.4

8h.5

8h.6

8h.7

8h.8

8h.9

8h.10

8h.11

8h.12

8h.14

8h.13

8h.15

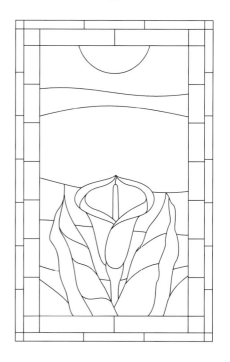

8h.16

8h.17

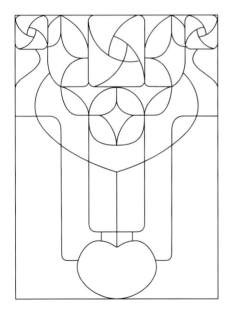

8h.18

8h.19

8h.20

8h.21

8h.22

8i.1

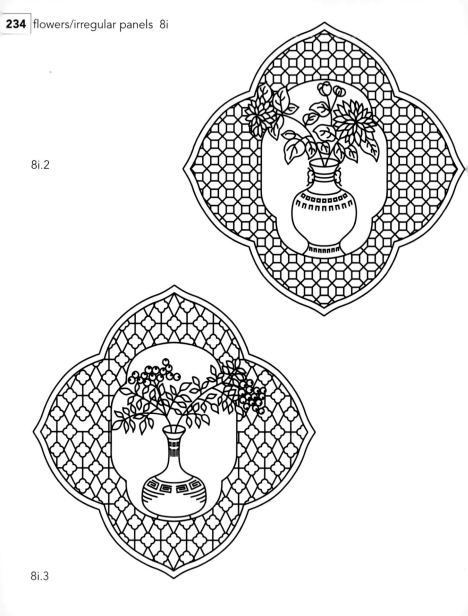

8i.2

8i.3

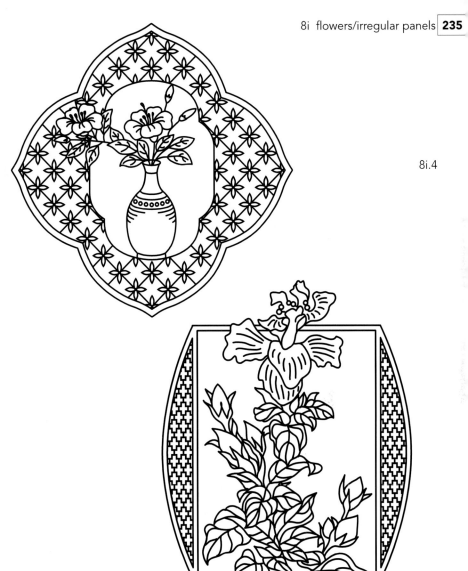

8i.4

8i.5

8i.6

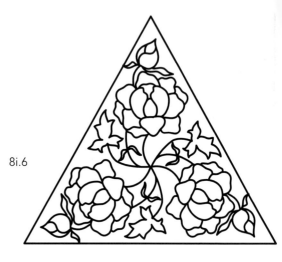

8i.7

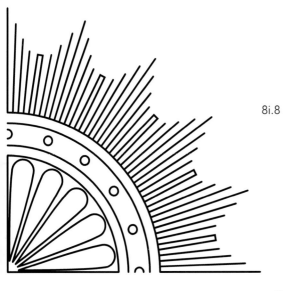

8i.8

8i.9

8i.10

8i.11

8i.12

8i.13

8i.14

8i.15

8i.16

8i.17

8j.1

8j.2

8j.3

8j.4

8j.5

8j.6

8j.7

8j.8

8j.9

8j.10

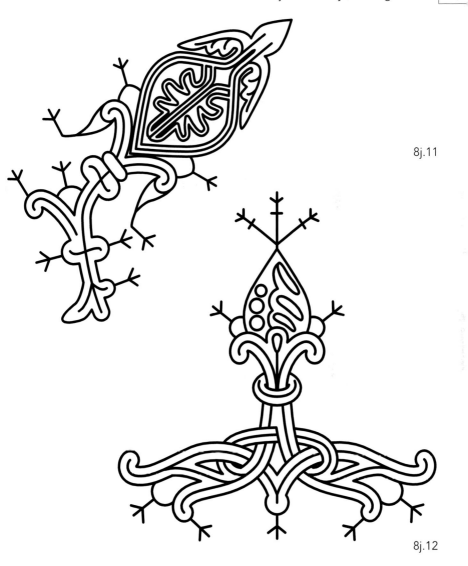

8j.11

8j.12

8j.14

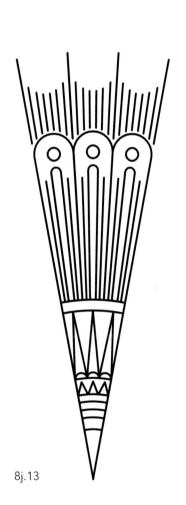

8j.13

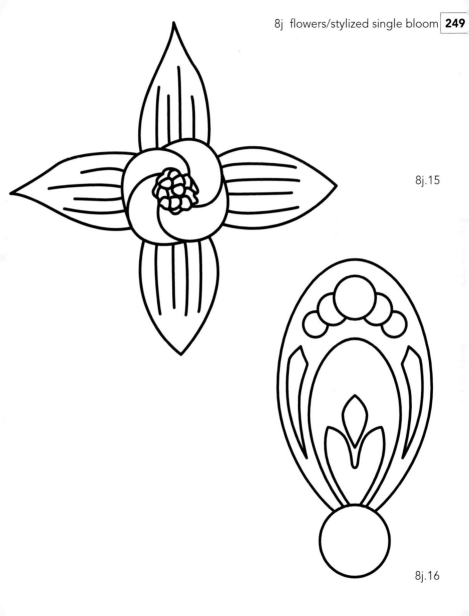

8j.15

8j.16

8j.17

8j.18

8j.19

8j.20

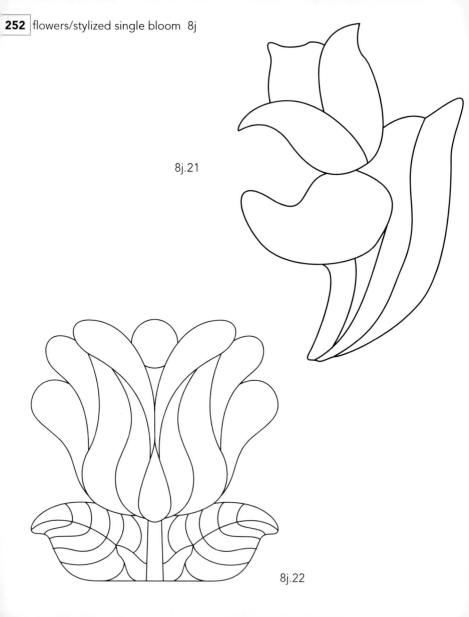

8j.21

8j.22

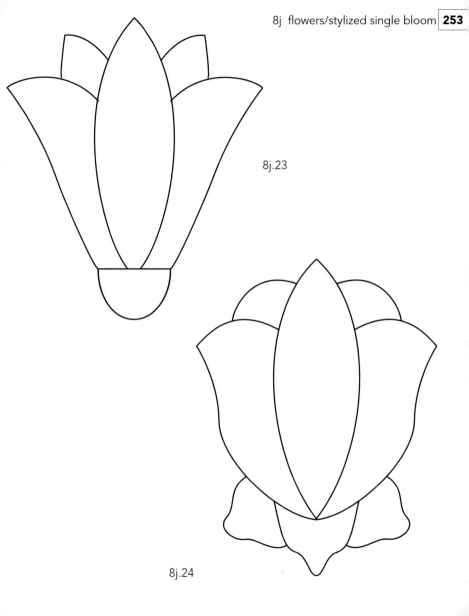

8j.23

8j.24

8k.1

8k.2

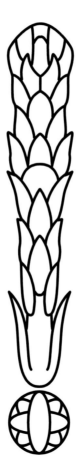

8k.3

8k.4

8k.5

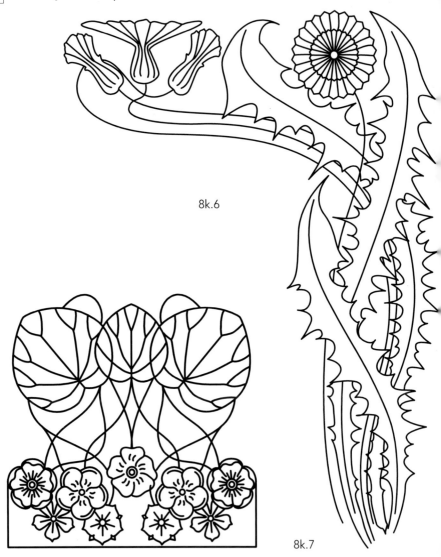

8k.6

8k.7

8k.8

8k.9

8k.10

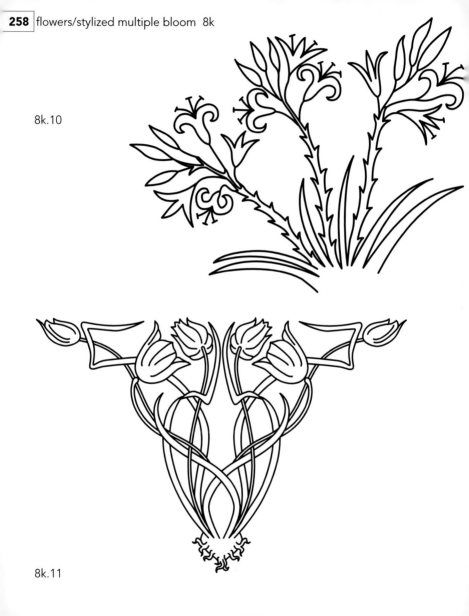

8k.11

8k.12

8k.13

8k.14

8k.15

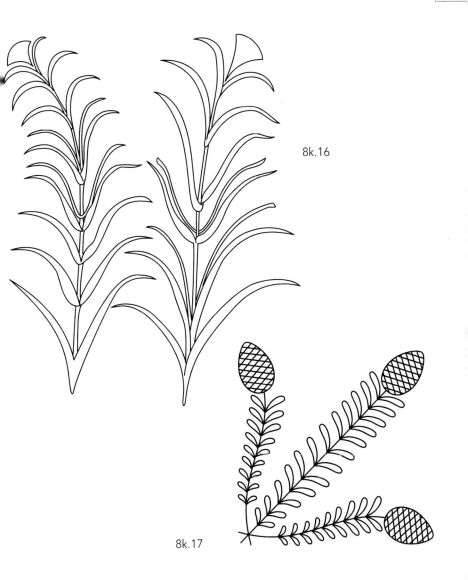

8k.16

8k.17

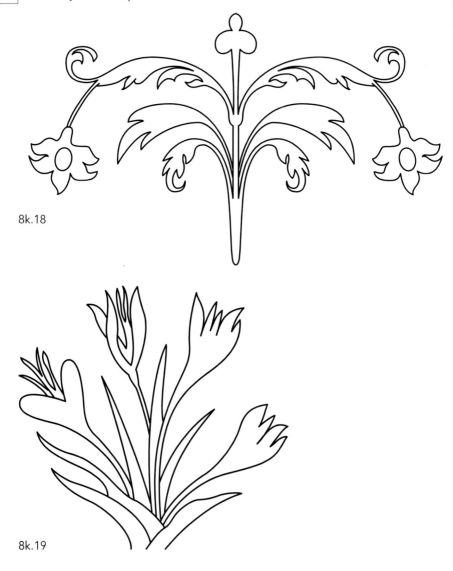

8k.18

8k.19

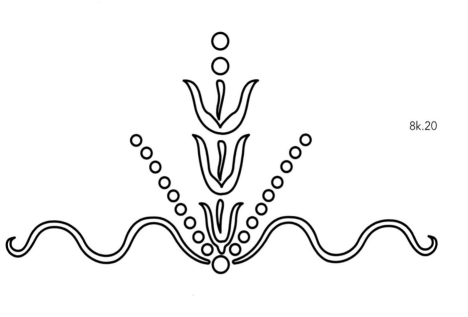

8k.20

8k.21

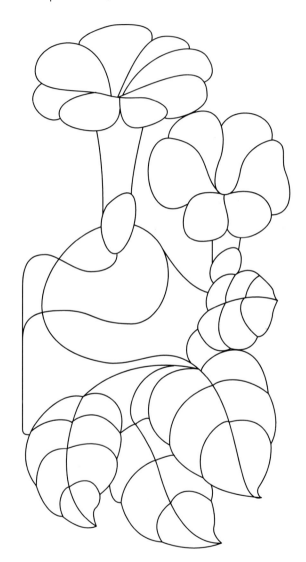

8k.23

8k.24

9.foliage

9a.1

9a.2

9a.3

9a.4

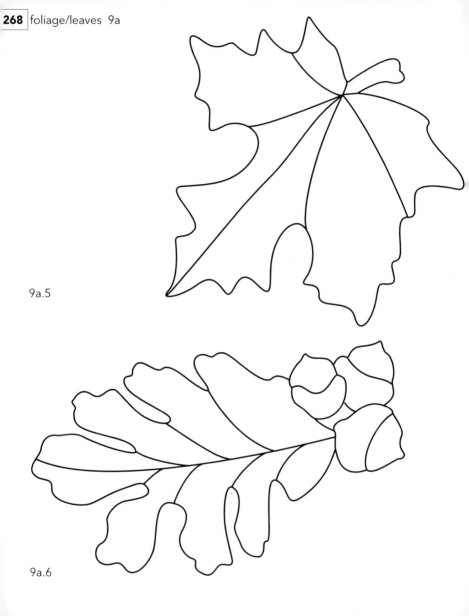

9a.5

9a.6

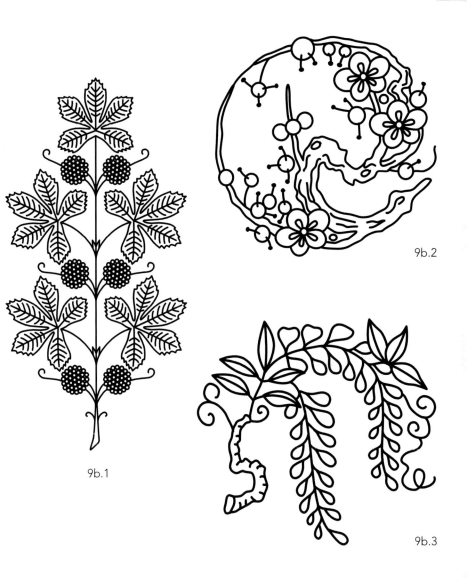

9b.2

9b.1

9b.3

9c.2

9c.1

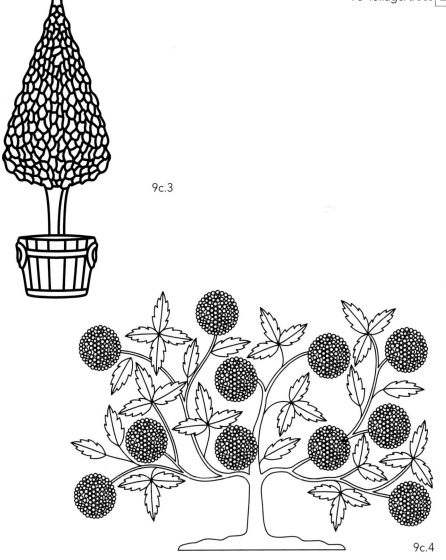

9c.3

9c.4

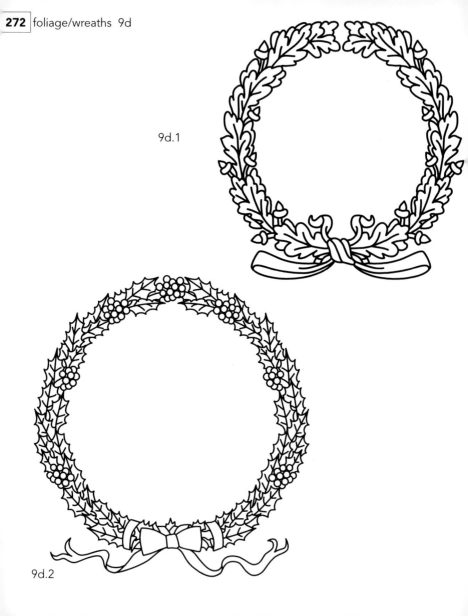

9d.1

9d.2

9d.3

9d.4

9e.1

9e.2

9e.3

9e.4

9f.1

9f.2

9f.3

9g.1

9g.2

9g.3

9g.4

9g.5

9h.1

9i.1

9i.2

9j.1

9j.2

9j.3

9j.4

9j.5

9j.6

9j.7

9j.8

9j.9

9j.10

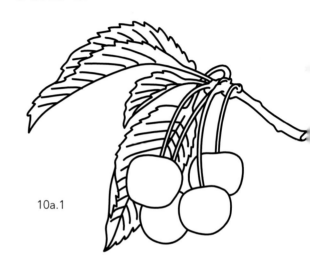

10a.1

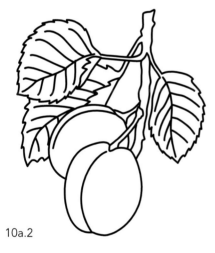

10a.2

10a.3

10a.4

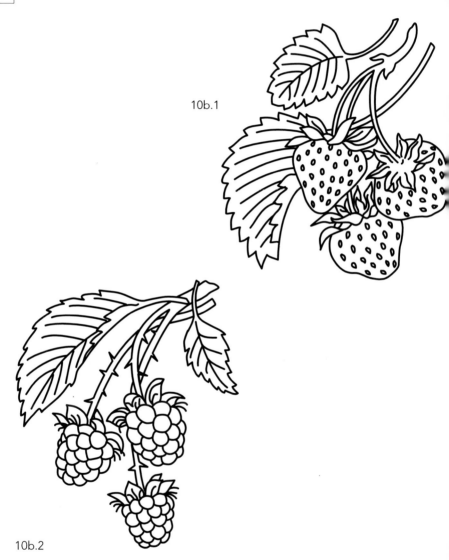

10b.1

10b.2

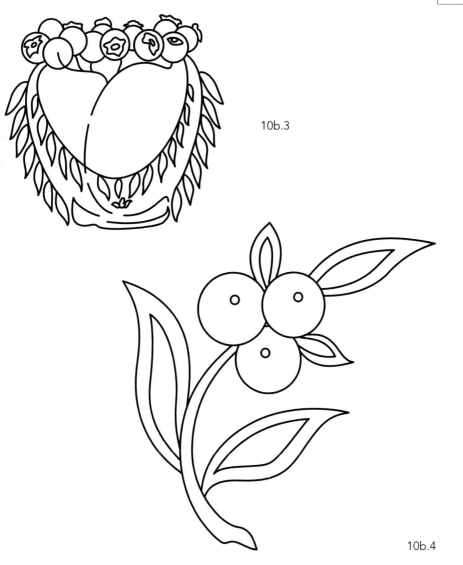

10b.3

10b.4

10b.5

10b.6

10c.1

10c.2

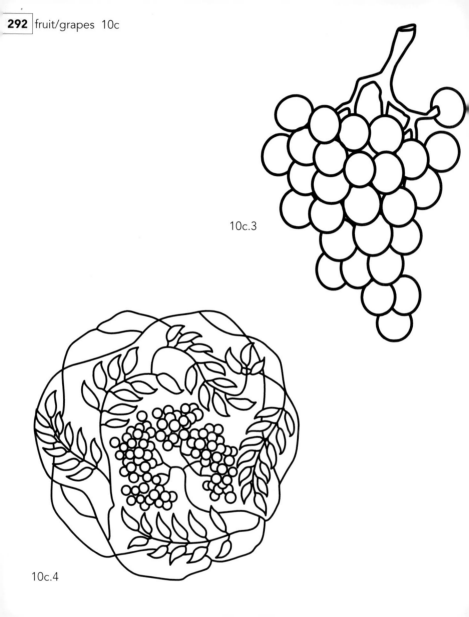

10c.3

10c.4

10d.1

10d.2

10d.3

10d.4

10d.5

10d.6

10e.1

10e.2

10e.3

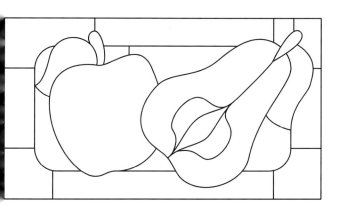

10f.1

10f.2

10f.3

10g.1

10g.2

10g.3

10g.4

10g.5

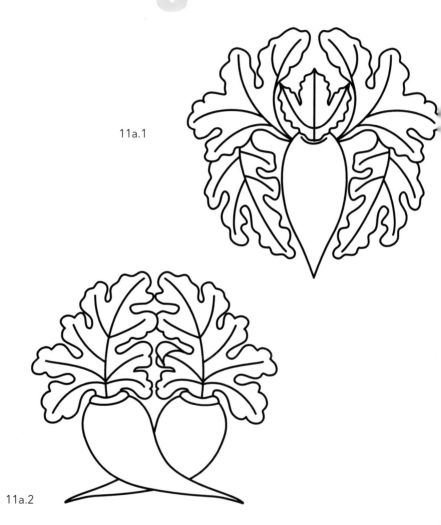

11a.1

11a.2

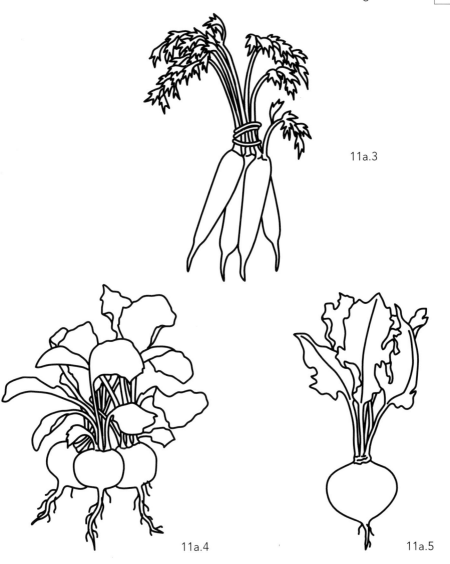

11a.3

11a.4

11a.5

11b.1

11b.2

11c.1

11c.2

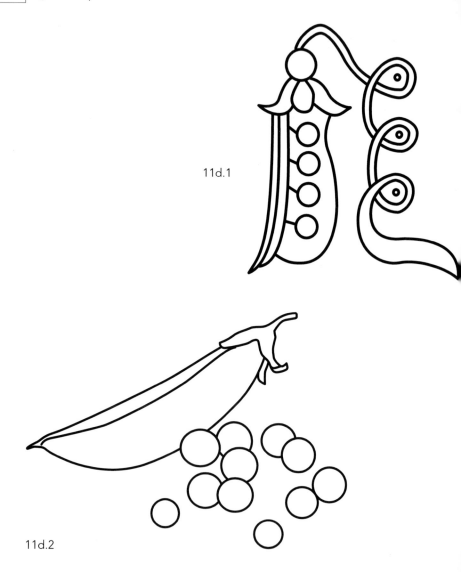

11d.1

11d.2

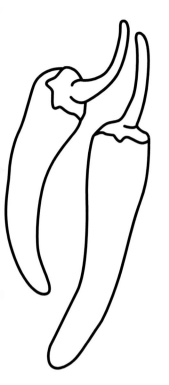

11e.1

11e.2

12.panels

12a.1

12a.2

12a.3

12a.4

12a.5

12a.6

12a.7

12a.8

12a.9

12b.1

12b.2

12b.3

12b.4

12b.5

12b.6

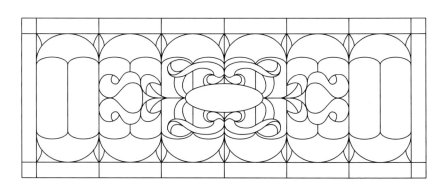

12c.1

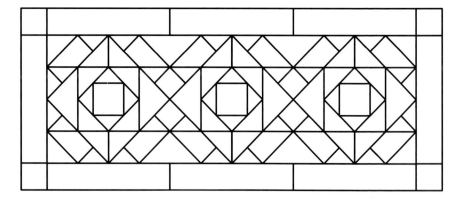

12c.2

12c.3

12c.4

12d.1

12d.2

12d.3

12d.4

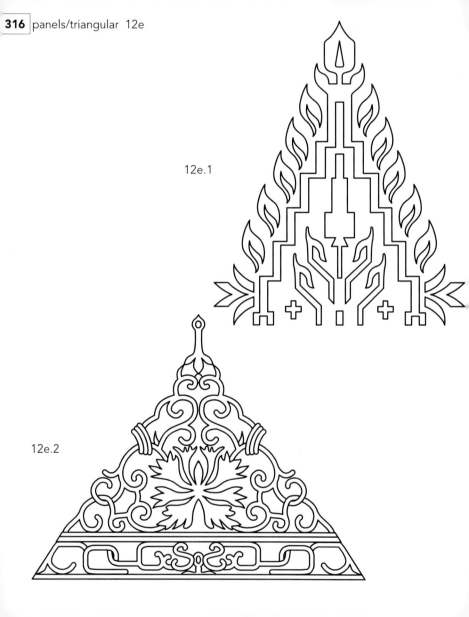

12e.1

12e.2

12f.1

12f.2

12f.3

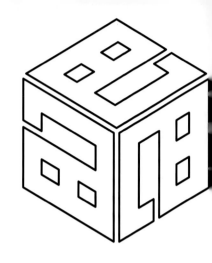

12f.4

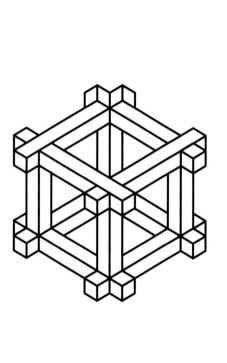

12f.5

12f.6

12g.1

12g.2

12g.3

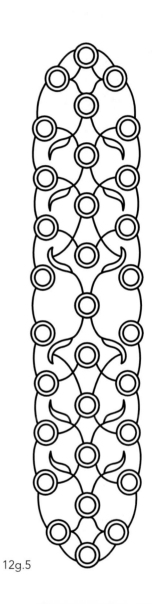

12g.4

12g.5

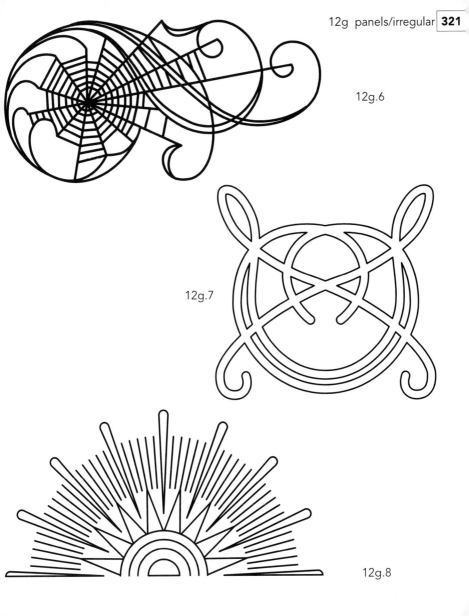

12g.6

12g.7

12g.8

12g.10

12g.9

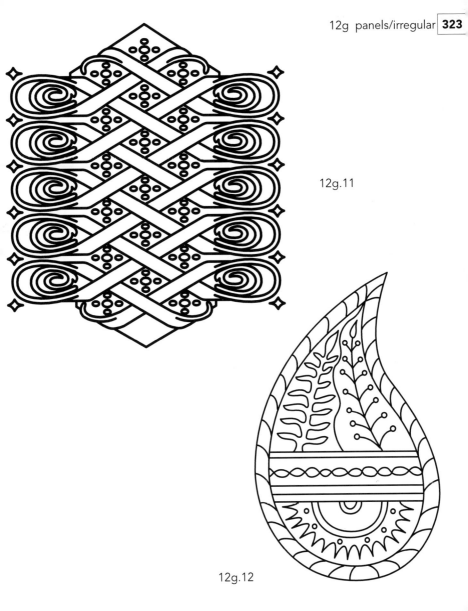

12g.11

12g.12

13.patterns

13a.1

13a.2

13a.3

13a.4

13a.5

13a.6

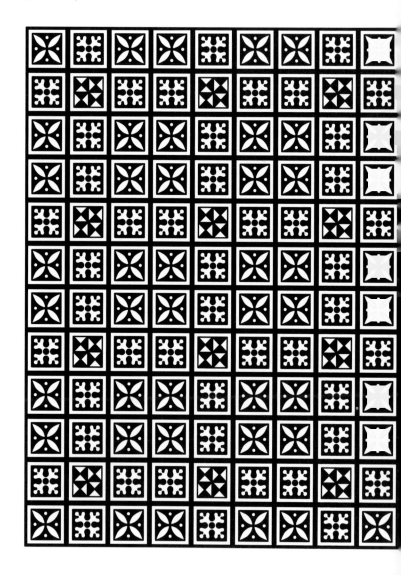

13a.7

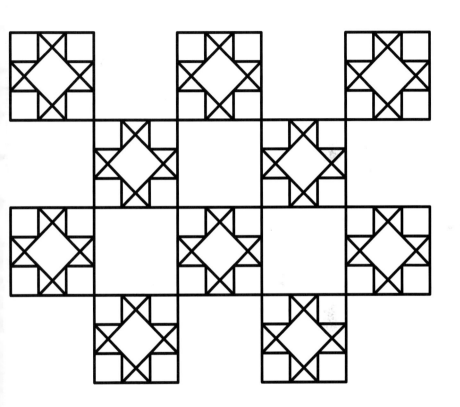

13a.8

13a.9

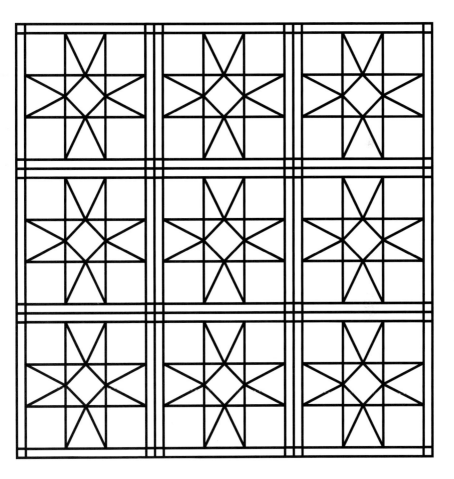

13a.10

13b.1

13b.2

13b.3

13b.4

13b.5

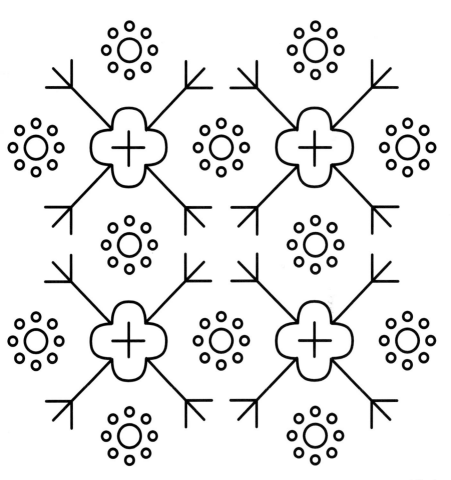

13b.6

13c.1

13c.2

13c.3

13c.4

13c.5

13c.6

13c.7

13c.8

13c.9

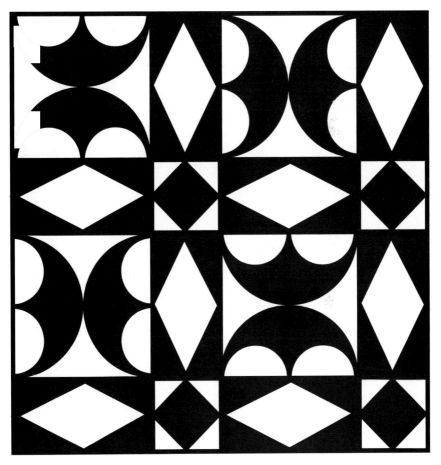

13c.10

13d.1

13d.2

13d.3

13d.4

13d.5

13d.6

13e.1

13e.2

13e.3

13e.4

13e.5

13e.6

13e.7

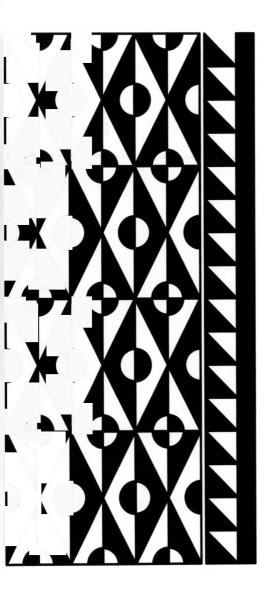

13e.8

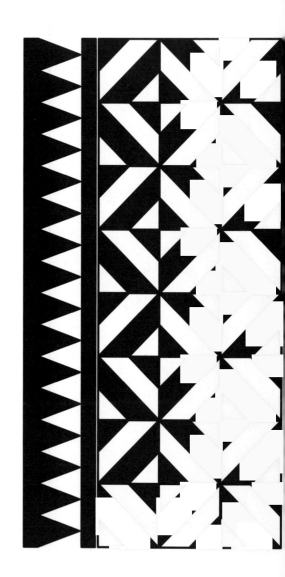

13e.9

13e.10

14.borders

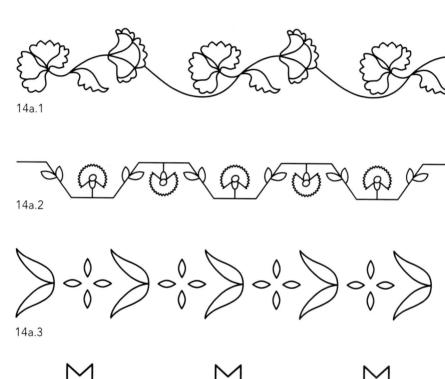

14a.1

14a.2

14a.3

14a.4

14a.5

14a.6

14a.7

14a.8

14a.9

14a.10

14a.11

14a.12

14a.13

14a.14

14a.15

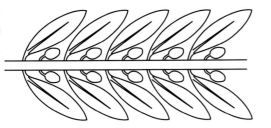

14b.1

14b.2

14b.3

14b.4

14b.5

14b.6

14b.7

14b.8

14b.9

14b.10

14c.1

14c.2

14c.3

14c.4

14c.5

14c.6

14c.7

14c.8

14c.9

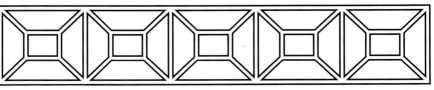

14d.1

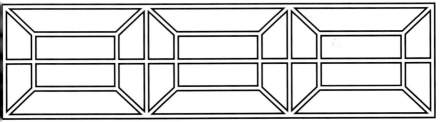

14d.2

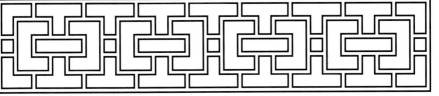

14d.3

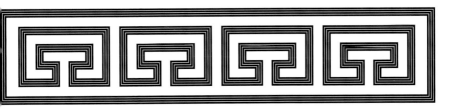

14d.4

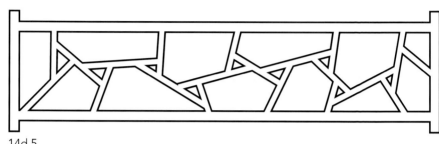

14d.5

14d.6

14d.7

14d.8

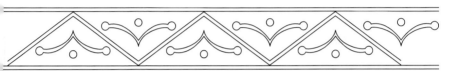

14d.9

14d.10

14e.1

14e.2

14e.3

14e.4

14e.5

14f.1

14f.2

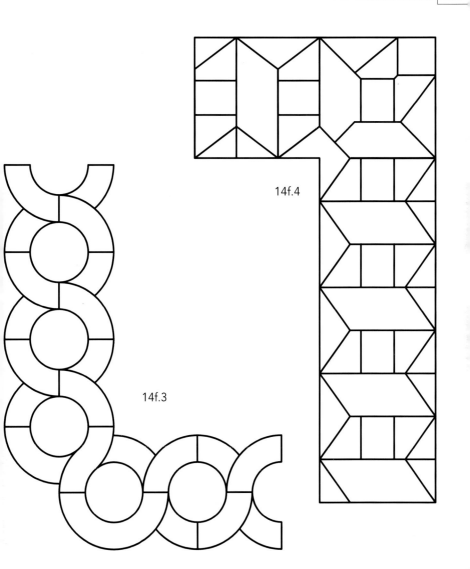

14f.4

14f.3

15a.1

15a.2

15a.3

15a.4

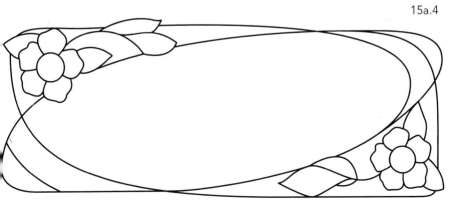

15a.5

15a.6

15a.7

15a.8

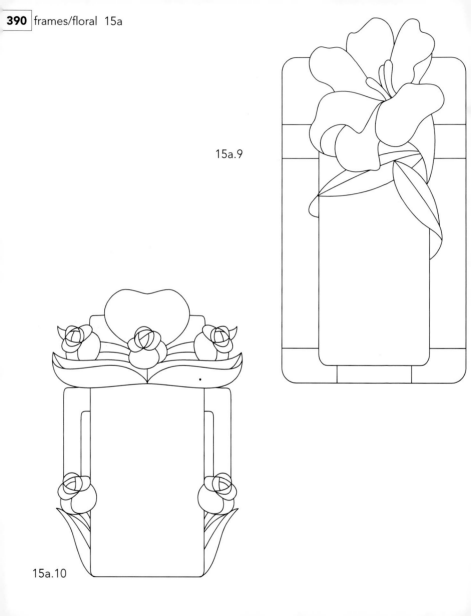

15a.9

15a.10

15a.11

15a.12

15a.13

15a.14

15b.1

15b.2

15b.3

15b.4

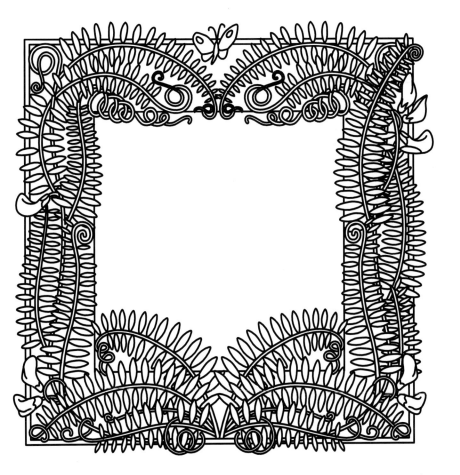

15b.5

15b.6

15b.7

15b.9

15b.8

15b.10

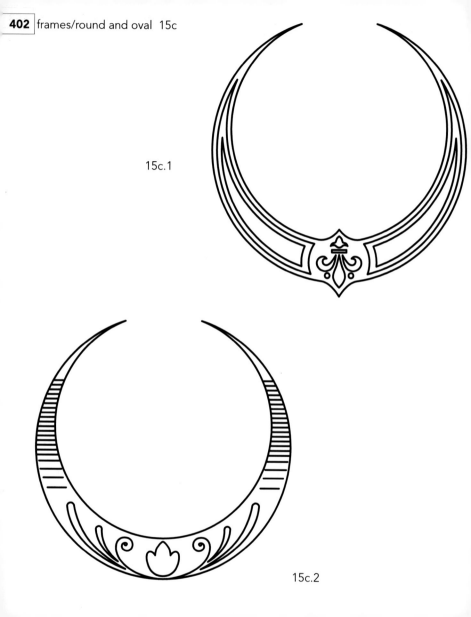

15c.1

15c.2

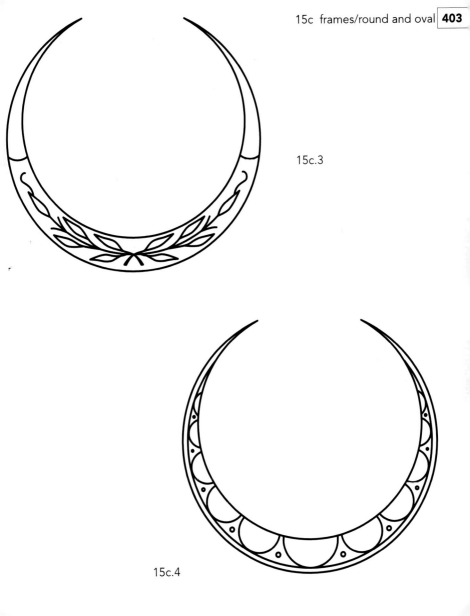

15c.3

15c.4

15c.5

15c.6

15c.7

15c.8

15c.9

15c.10

15c.11

15d.1

15d.2

15d.3

15e.1

15e.2

15e.3

15e.4

15e.5

15e.6

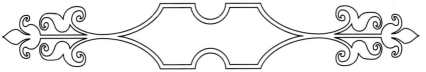

15e.7

15e.9

15e.10

15e.11

15e.12

18.banners

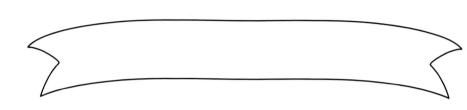

16a.1

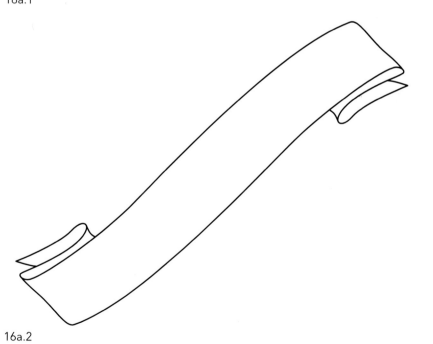

16a.2

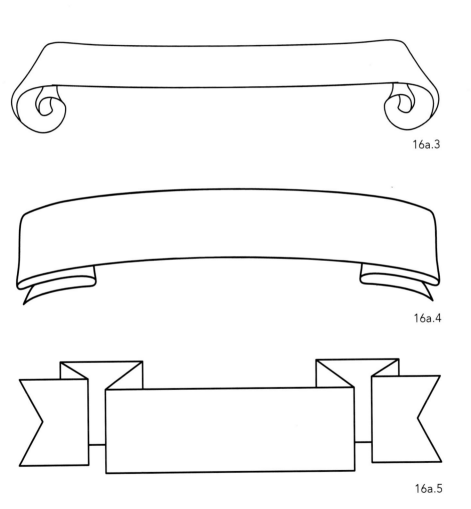

16a.3

16a.4

16a.5

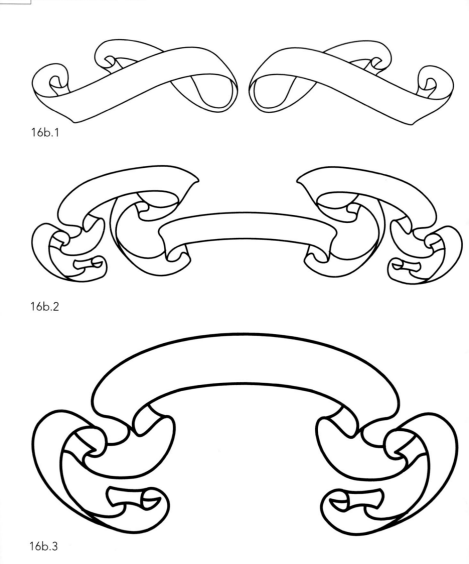

16b.1

16b.2

16b.3

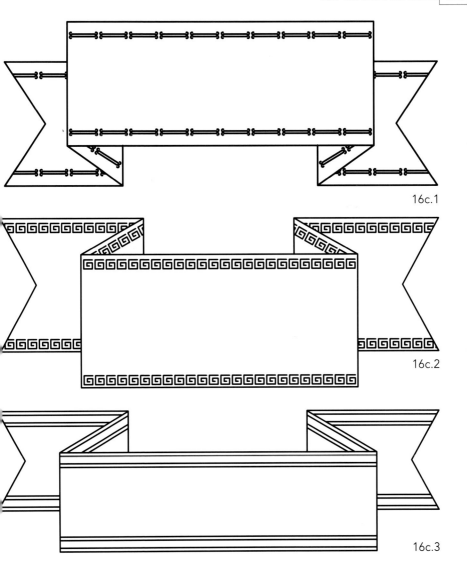

16c.1

16c.2

16c.3

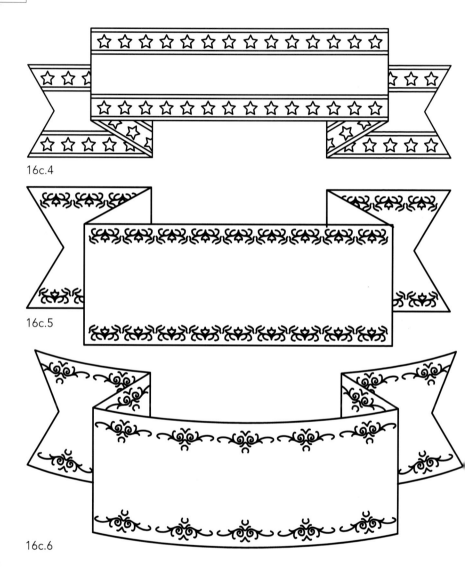

16c.4

16c.5

16c.6

16d.1

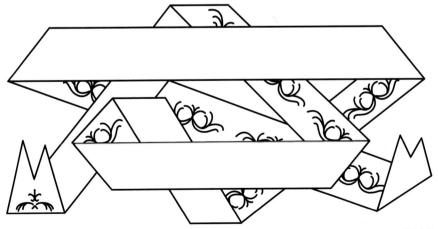

16d.2

17a.1

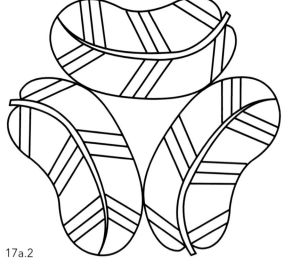

17a.2

17a.3

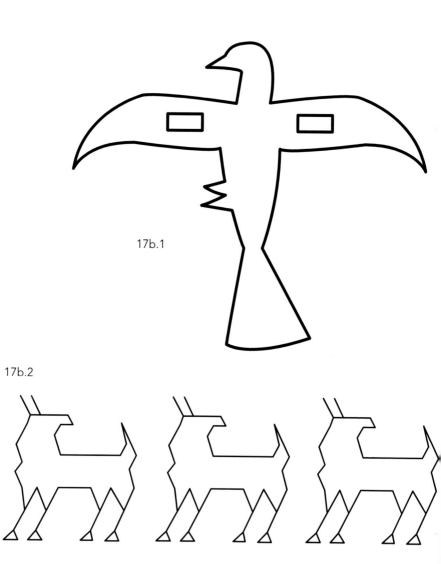

17b.1

17b.2

17c.1

17c.2

17d.1

17d.2

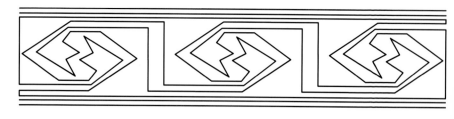

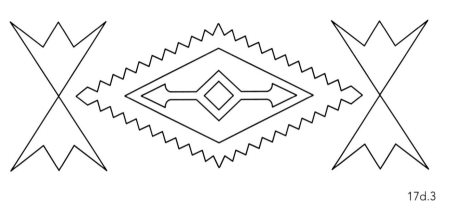

17d.3

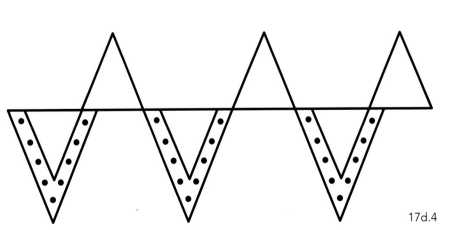

17d.4

17d.5

17d.6

17d.7

17d.8

17e.1

17e.2

17e.3

17e.4

17e.5

17e.6

17e.7

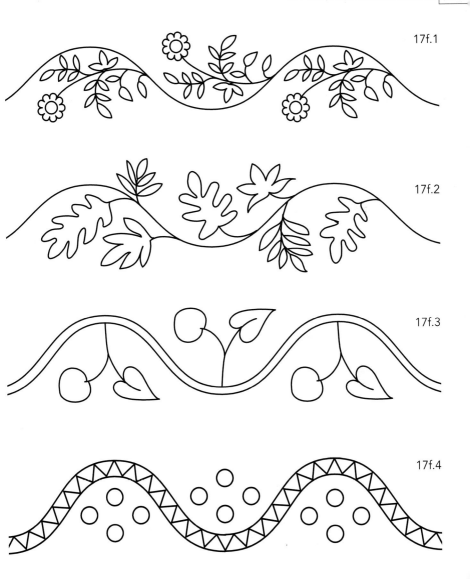

17f.1

17f.2

17f.3

17f.4

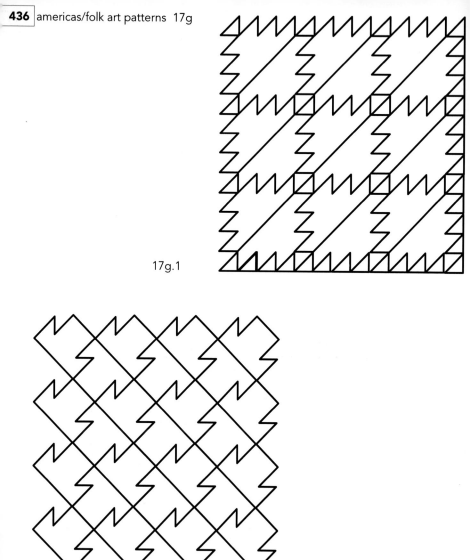

17g.1

17g.2

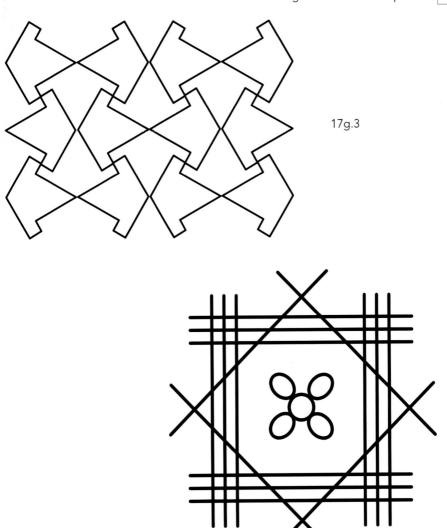

17g.3

17g.4

17h.1

17h.2

17h.3

17h.4

17h.5

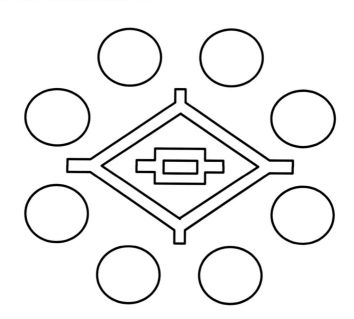

17i.1

17i.2

17i.3

17i.4

17i.5

17i.6

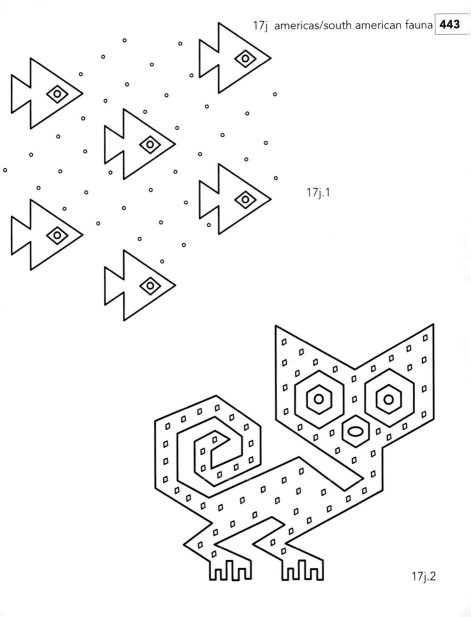

17j.1

17j.2

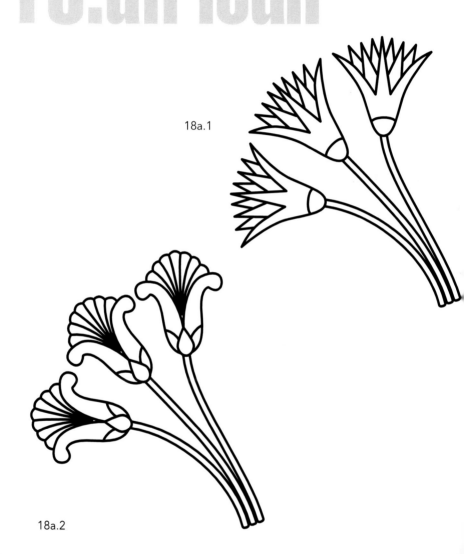

18a.1

18a.2

18a.3

18a.4

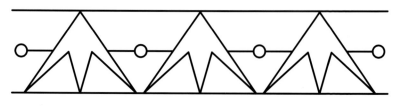

18b.1

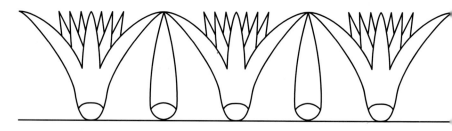

18b.2

18b.3

18b.4

18b.5

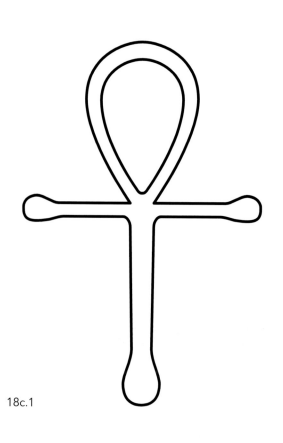

18c.1

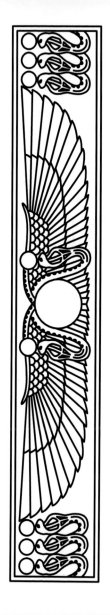

18c.2

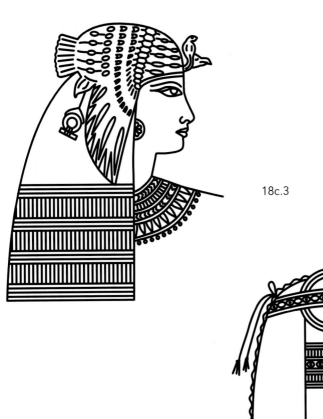

18c.3

18c.4

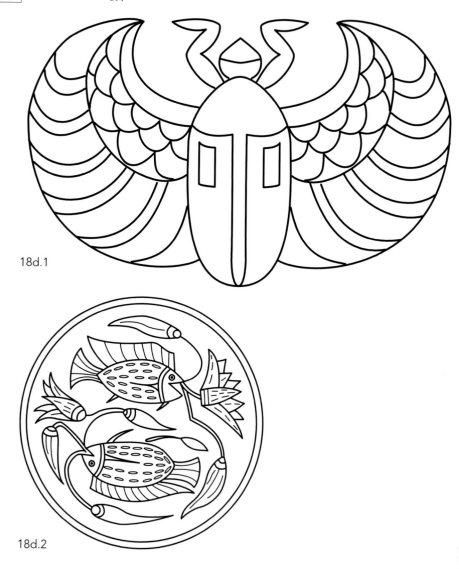

18d.1

18d.2

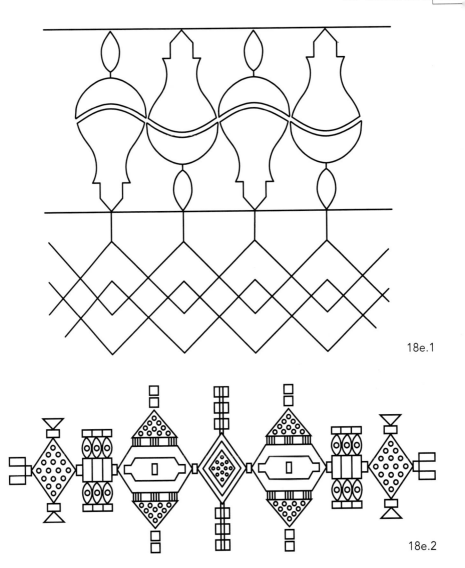

18e.1

18e.2

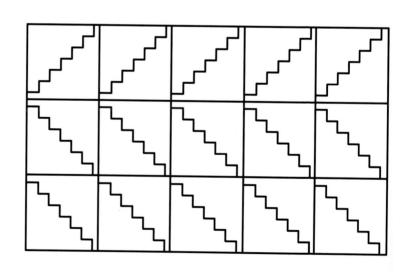

18e.3

18e.4

18e.5

18e.6

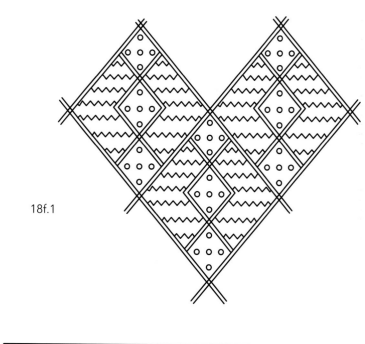

18f.1

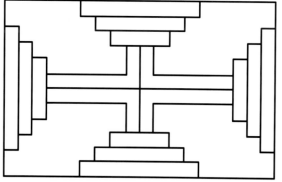

18f.2

18f.3

18f.4

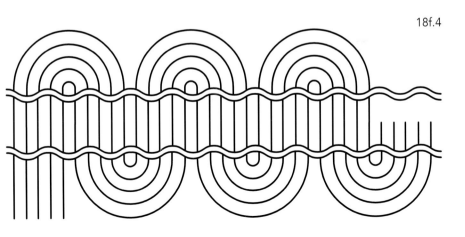

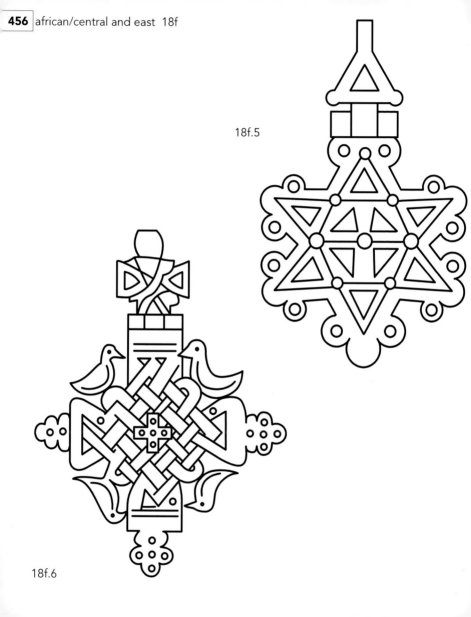

18f.5

18f.6

18g.1

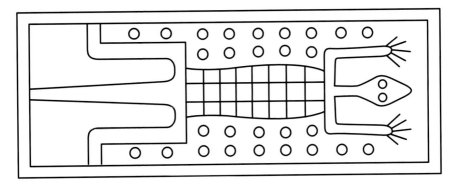

18g.2

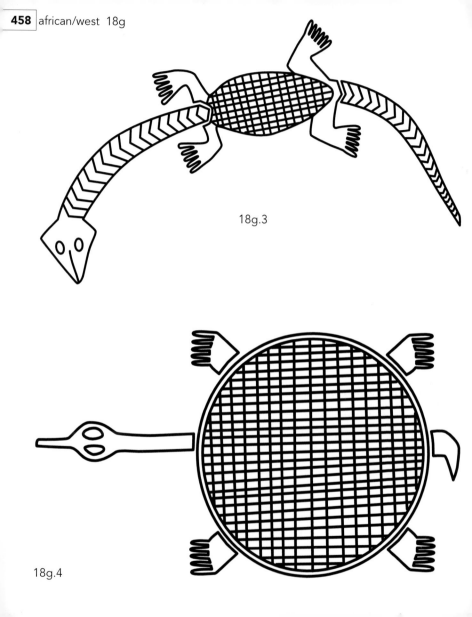

18g.3

18g.4

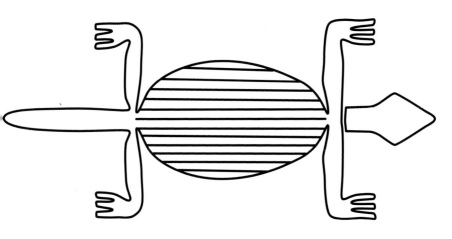

18g.5

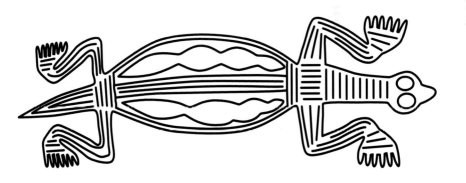

18g.6

19a.1

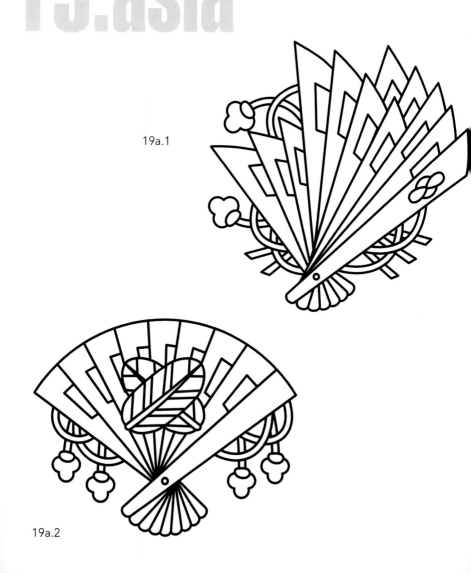

19a.2

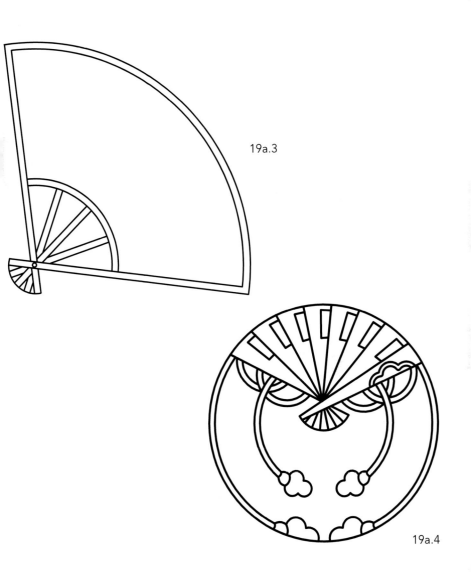

19a.3

19a.4

19b.1

19b.2

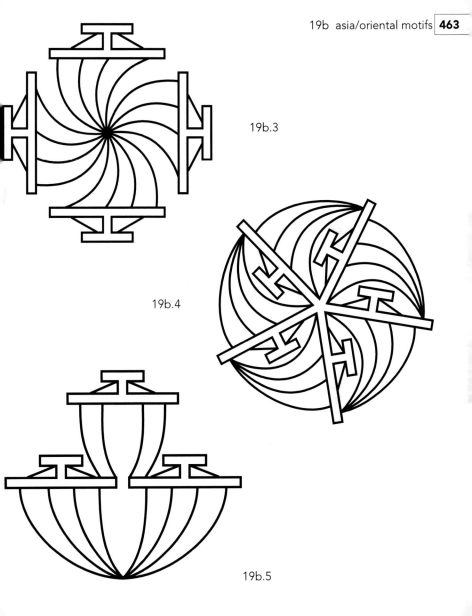

19b.3

19b.4

19b.5

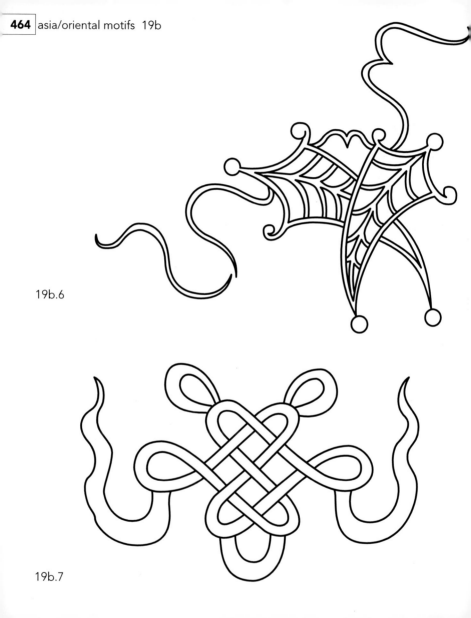

19b.6

19b.7

19c.1

19c.2

19c.3

19c.4

19d.1

19e.1

19e.2

19e.3

19f.1

19f.2

19f.3

19g.1

19h.1

19h.2

19h.3

19i.1

19i.2

19i.3

19i.4

19i.5

19j.2

19j.1

19k.1

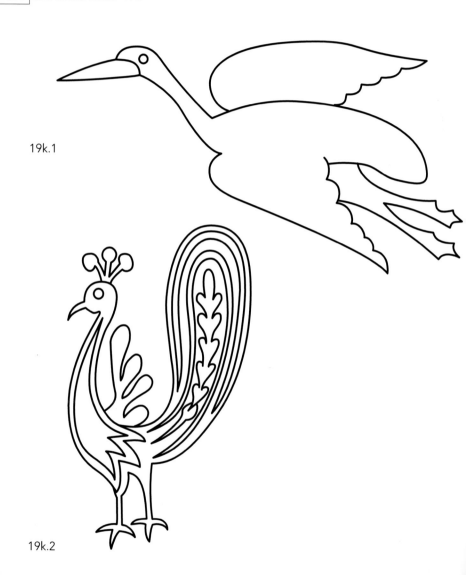

19k.2

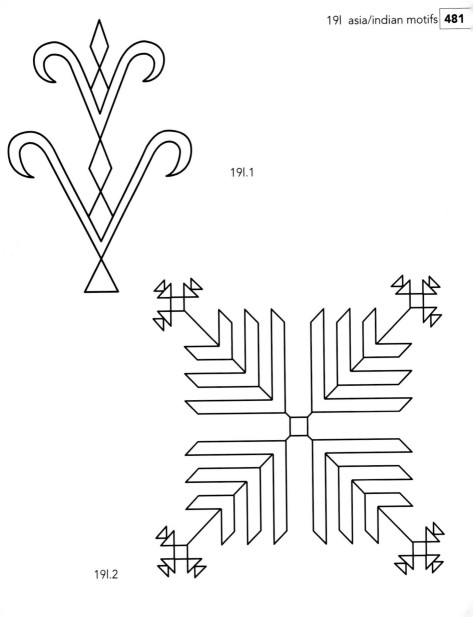

19l.1

19l.2

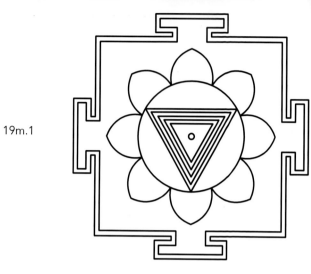

19m.1

19m.2

19m.3

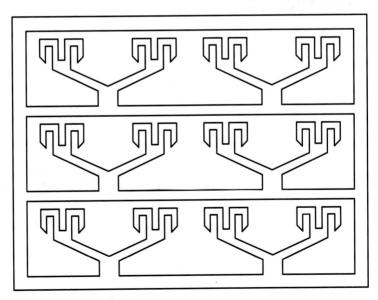

19m.4

19n.1

19n.2

19n.3

19n.4

19n.5

19n.6

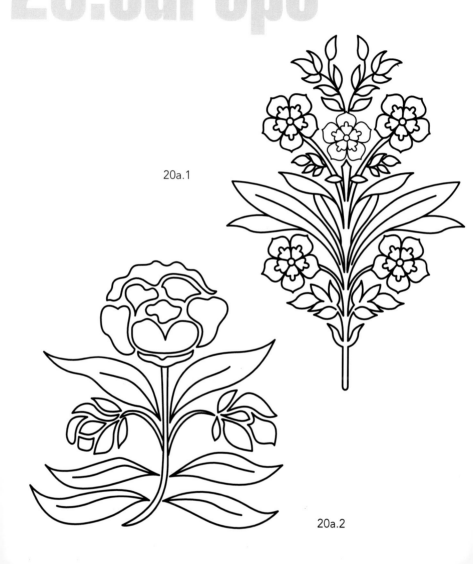

20a.1

20a.2

20b.1

20b.2

20b.3

20b.4

20c.1

20c.2

20d.1

20d.2

20d.3

20d.4

20e.1

20e.2

20e.3

20e.4

20f.1

20f.2

20f.3

20f.4

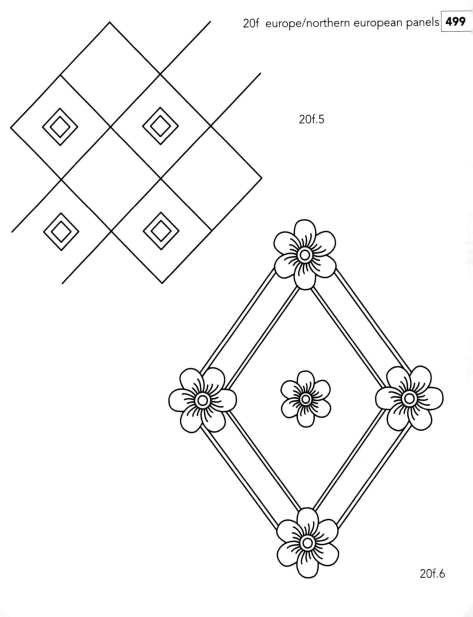

20f.5

20f.6

20f.7

20f.8

20f.9

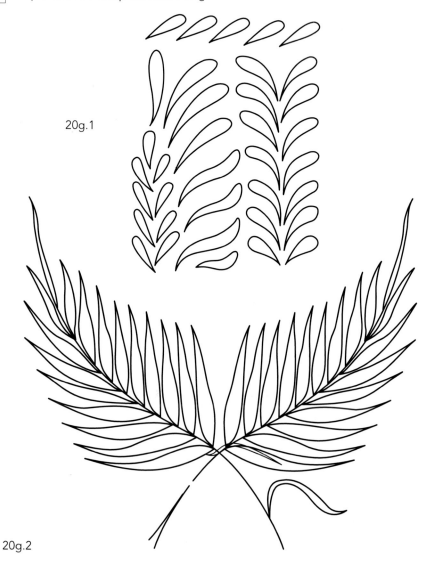

20g.1

20g.2

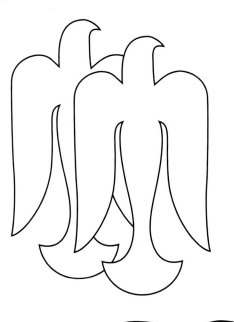

20h.1

20h.2

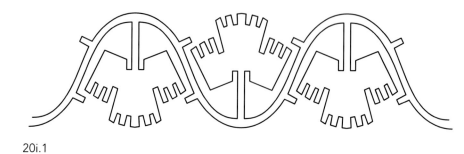

20i.1

20i.2

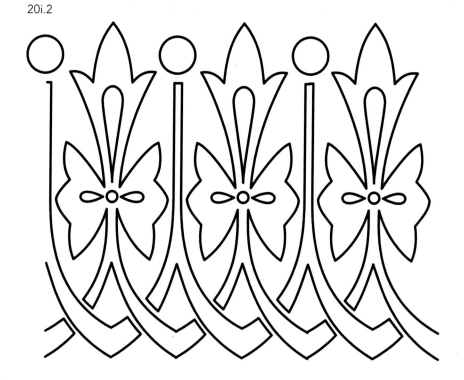

20i.3

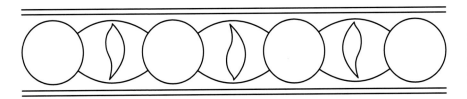

20i.4

20i.5

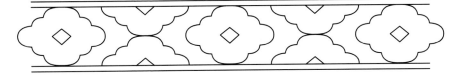

20j.1

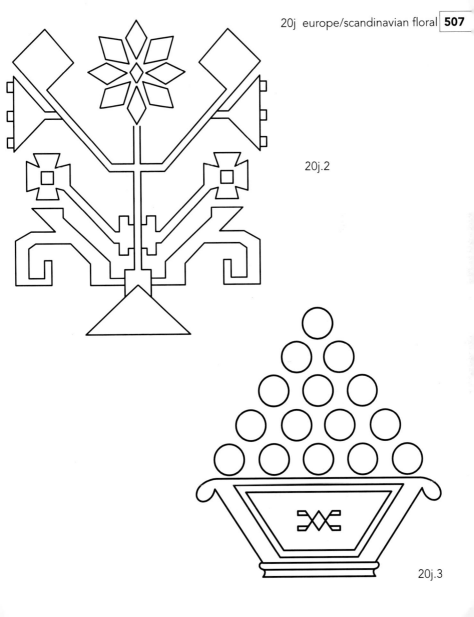

20j.2

20j.3

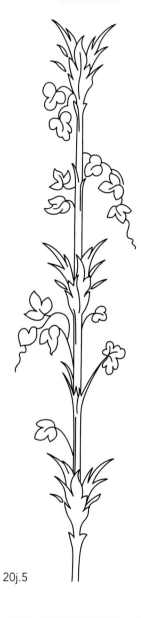

20j.4

20j.5

20k.1

20k.2

20k.3

Some of the
illustrations in this
book are taken from
*The Crafter's Pattern
Sourcebook* by
Mary MacCarthy
(Collins & Brown).